STRANGE WORLD

BY FRANK EDWARDS

My First 10,000,000 *Sponsors*
Strangest of All
Stranger Than Science
Strange People

By FRANK EDWARDS

STRANGE WORLD

CITADEL PRESS · Secaucus, New Jersey

To my sisters
Leona and Frances

Table of Contents

Table of Contents

Table of Contents

PART ONE

. . . Science as an interpreter of the mysteries of the Universe is a dismal failure.

—Israel Zangwill (1864-1926)

1

She Dreamed a Headline

The big four-engined Constellation swept down over the water and leveled off for the landing strip only a hundred feet away. The plane struck the water, bounced, hooked a wing into the earth and cartwheeled—a ball of flames.

Mrs. John Walik of Long Beach awoke with a start.

It was a little past three in the morning of January 29, 1963. She had been having a nightmare, but she realized with a shiver that the plane she had seen in the dream was identical to the one in which her husband was employed as a navigator. He was then on a cargo trip for Slick Airways, flying in a Constellation in which he had made many flights previously; but just where he was, or whether he was safe, Mrs. Walik did not know. She did know, however, that the dream of that plane crash had been unusually vivid and she could not dismiss it from her mind.

She phoned the Slick Airways office that morning, trying to check on John Walik's whereabouts—and, of course, on his well-being. The office could only tell her that no plane crashes had been reported; the Constellation on which

John was working was somewhere in the eastern part of the country delivering a load of freight and was due back to the West Coast in a few days.

Try as she might, Mrs. Walik could not rid herself of the gnawing dread that her dream was a prelude to disaster. She told friends and neighbors about it and, of course, she told her own family. Most of them shrugged it off. Some of them laughed at her fears. But none of them forgot that she had described a certain type of plane involved in a particular type of accident.

The sequel to her nightmare made headlines on February 4, 1963. The LONG BEACH INDEPENDENT PRESS headline said: "Mate's Plane Crash Seen in Wife's Dream."

Nagged by her memory of that nightmare, Mrs. Walik had become increasingly restive. On Sunday morning, February 3, 1963, she could no longer stand it, and she again called the office of the airline for which John Walik worked. They told her that there had been no trouble—in fact, her husband's plane was due in at the San Francisco International Airport that same morning.

Mrs. Walik hung up the phone with a sigh of relief. But it was short-lived. She suddenly realized that San Francisco International Airport is approached over the Bay—and in her dream she had seen the plane strike the water before it struck the earth.

Had something gone wrong after all?

She phoned the airline office in San Francisco—and she was on the line with them when her husband's plane struck the field and burst into flames. Five of the crewmen died; four others, including her husband, survived the crash.

There was but one major discrepancy between the dream and the actual crash. In the dream she had distinctly seen the plane glance off the water at the edge of the airport; in reality the plane did not strike the water but crashed beside the runway and caught fire.

As the Long Beach paper said of the incident: "It was the plane crash she had seen in her dreams five days before it happened!"

2

Midgets from Mars?

Because the expression "little green men" has been used satirically to describe possible creatures from other worlds, reports of little humanoid creatures seen around presumed space craft have been treated with great caution. Nevertheless, many credible witnesses have reported seeing such creatures—and the reports have come from widely separated parts of the world. Furthermore, the descriptions have shown such remarkable similarity in detail that the chance that they were all fraudulent is virtually nil.

Dr. Hermann Oberth, the great German rocket scientist who investigated the so-called "flying saucers" for the West German government, is one of those who has expressed the conviction that the Unidentified Flying Objects (UFO's) are intelligently conceived and controlled.

Since the majority of the UFO's are disc-shaped things about twenty-five feet in diameter with a five- or six-foot-high dome in the center, it stands to reason that if the operators are in the dome they must be comparatively small in stature.

Testimony indicates that they are.

On the morning of November 28, 1954, Gustavo Gonzales and his helper, José Ponce, left Caracas in a truck bound for Petare, about twenty minutes distant. Time, 2 A.M.

According to the sworn testimony they later filed with police, the men had gone about one-third of the distance to Petare when they came around a sharp bend in the road and found their way blocked by a luminous, hemispherical object which was suspended four or five feet above the road.

Gonzales and Ponce got out of their truck to have a better look at this unusual craft. Gonzales made the mistake of grabbing a small "man" who ran toward him. He later told police that he intended to turn the fellow over to the law for blocking the road—and he added that he was surprised at the light weight of the creature— which he estimated at not more than thirty-five pounds. The little fellow is described as wearing nothing but a sort of light brown loin cloth and was dark of skin and covered with short bristly hair.

Gonzales had more than he could handle. He found himself flung about fifteen feet. Ponce took off for the police station, a block and a half away. As Ponce ran, he saw two other little manlike creatures running toward the shiny craft, carrying what appeared to be plants of some sort which they had evidently pulled up by the roots.

Gonzales was bloodied and half-stunned by his fall, but when the little creature came toward him he pulled his knife and struck the fellow's shoulder. The knife glanced off without effect. Something struck Gonzales at that point but he managed to get away, stumbling toward the police station. When the two men told their story, they were suspected of being drunk; however, medical tests showed that not only were they stone sober, but both were suffering from shock. They were given sedatives and allowed to rest before making their sworn statements.

Corroboration of their strange tale came from a surprising source. Two days after the incident, one of the medical doctors who had examined Gonzales and Ponce admitted that he had been an eyewitness to this strange encounter as he returned home from an emergency call. He had stayed only long enough to ascertain what was taking place; then he hurried from the scene lest he become involved in some undesirable publicity. But because of the evident nature and importance of the incident, he decided to confirm the men's story, provided the Caracas officials kept his identity secret.

Nor was this the only account of the sort to emanate from Venezuela; for South America was the scene of countless visitations by Unidentified Flying Objects. On May 7, 1955, the Caracas daily, EL UNIVERSAL, reported the bizarre story of a prominent engineer who told of finding a disc-shaped craft sitting in a field beside the highway in isolated Bahia Blanca in Argentina. A blinking light was flashing atop the shallow dome on the craft. A small door was open on the side and the engineer squeezed in.

He told authorities that he found three small men in a circular enclosure. They were dressed in tightly fitting brown coverall-type garments. One was seated at a control desk, the other two were lying on short curved lounges. All were dead. He estimated them to be not more than four feet tall, with dark brown skin and yellowish eyes.

The engineer took friends back with him to the spot; but by the time they got there the craft was gone. They made pictures of it—or a similar object—overhead. The only tangible evidence they secured was some small heaps of grayish material which was hot to the touch. They turned the material over to the government, by request, and were unable to learn what it was or what became of it.

From Sweden the newspapers carried accounts of an encounter which two young men experienced on December 20, 1958, shortly before three in the morning. On their way home from a dance, they stopped to investigate a huge glowing object in a clearing in the woods near the highway. The men, one a twenty-five-year-old truck driver and the other a thirty-year-old student, got close enough to see a disc-shaped craft of some sort standing about three feet above the earth on short metal legs. Then, they told authorities, they were grabbed by four grayish or grayclad creatures about four feet tall. The student managed to tear loose and reach the car, where he began to blow the horn frantically in hope of securing help. The truck driver was fighting as best he could, but found himself no match for his little adversaries. He was able to wrap his arms around a metal highway sign from which they could not loosen his grip. After a struggle which lasted from four to seven minutes, according to the estimate of the two young men, their antagonists suddenly fled from the scene and the luminous craft sped away into the night, leaving the men to make their way into Halsingborg.

Said Hans Gustavsson, the truck driver: "The one thing I can never forget about this terrible experience is the sickening smell of those creatures. It haunts me!"

From the village of Quaroubles, France, came the report of thirty-four-year-old Marius Dewilde, an employee at the Blanc Misseron metal works plant. The date was September 10, 1954, and the clock had just struck 10:30 P.M. when Dewilde heard his dog barking frantically outside his little house, located near a railroad track. Suspecting thieves, Dewilde picked up his flashlight and slipped out through the back door.

In the darkness he could dimly make out some sort of massive object on or near the railroad tracks, and he could hear movement in that general direction. The dog came crawling to Dewilde, and just at that moment he heard footsteps. He told authorities later that since he lives on the border between France and Belgium, he suspected that smugglers were about. A moment later Dewilde got the shock of his life; for he flashed on his light and in its beam stood two tiny creatures like very small men in shiny divers' suits, with large glass or plastic helmets over their heads. As he lunged to slam the garden gate to prevent their escape, he found himself pinned in the brilliant white beam of light from the object on the railroad tracks. He was dazzled by the glare—and seemed unable to move. When it went out, seconds later, the little creatures were gone—as was the object itself.

Subsequent investigation by French authorities revealed that something of considerable weight had been resting on the wooden crossties (known as ballast planks to French railroaders). The marks were regularly spaced and were fresh—on tracks where no work had been done for months. Some of the stones in the roadbed were so burned that they crumbled to the touch—but that was all the tangible evidence that had been left by the object and its strange little operators.

One Herr Lincke, former Mayor of Hasselbach, Germany, reported to authorities that he and his teen-age daughter watched a shiny disc-shaped craft land in a clearing near the woods where they had stopped to rest on their bicycle trip. The sworn testimony of the ex-Mayor and his daughter included a description of the "little men" which was markedly similar to other descriptions from other parts of the world: Three to three-and-a-half feet tall, clad in shiny coverall type garments, with helmets and, in this case, with blue lights attached to the fronts of their garments. They were watched for several minutes in daylight before they clambered back into the craft and rose out of sight.

From the house magazine of the Steep Rock Iron Mines, Ltd., of Steep Rock Lake, Ontario, comes one of the most interesting and definitive accounts of this sort. It originally appeared in that publication in September and October of 1950 and was subsequently reprinted in many Canadian newspapers.

Summarized, it recounted the experience reported by a mining engineer and his wife which took place on July 2, 1950, shortly before dusk.

They had driven to a portion of Steep Rock Lake known as Sawbill Bay, a remote and secluded cove. Their car was parked under the trees and was thus well out of sight. They were making some tea over a little fire when the air suddenly began to vibrate, as though there had been blasting nearby. Unable to locate the source of the disturbance, the engineer climbed up on a rock which overlooked the bay.

Through a cleft near the top of the giant boulder he could see a shiny craft of some sort resting on the surface of the water about six hundred yards away. His wife scrambled up beside him and together they watched the object for a total of perhaps ten minutes.

In their testimony they agreed that hatch covers opened in the low dome on top of the craft and several (eight or nine) small, manlike creatures appeared through the hatches. The couple estimated the craft to be forty to fifty feet in diameter, flat on the bottom, with a dome fifteen feet high inside a rim that was about ten feet wide. The little creatures appeared to be men less than four feet tall, and all except one were wearing bright blue skull caps. The exception was one who wore a red skull cap, or helmet, and this one was visible only from the chest up, in a hatch on top of the dome.

The creatures moved jerkily—almost mechanically—the couple reported to authorities. Several of them shoved a bright green hose or tube into the water and, after a few minutes of this, the creatures all scrambled inside, closed the hatches, and the craft rose straight into the air, changing color from mixed rose and blue to a dazzling white as it picked up speed. It was out of sight in approximately twenty seconds.

From Africa, Europe, South America, and North America the eyewitness reports of these craft and their tiny passengers have come in. For that matter, the reports continue to come in.

In the Hobart, Tasmania, MERCURY for February 5, 1963, there is the interesting account which is headlined:

"Helmeted Man Seen By Object"

Midgets From Mars?

The article says: "A woman from the Adelaide suburb of Norwood told yesterday of an illuminated oval-shaped object which landed near Salisbury.

"Mrs. E. D. Silvester, a high school teacher, told authorities that she and her three children had watched a luminous, oval-shaped object on the ground for about ten minutes before it took off. The witnesses all agreed on the appearance of a very small man or humanoid creature who was walking around beside the object. The creature appeared (to the witnesses) to be wearing a shiny helmet of some sort, with tanks or breathing apparatus on his back.

"Mrs. Silvester said the children with her first spotted the object settling to earth as she drove along the Salisbury-Elizabeth road. She stopped her automobile and from a point about 200 yards from the object the four of them watched it and its strange occupant for about ten minutes, the teacher told authorities."

Little humanoid creatures seen in and around the Unidentified Flying Objects in all parts of the world . . . strange craft that have eluded our jets with ease and visited every important military and communications center on earth . . . a world-wide pattern of official silence which has still not been able to conceal the true nature and extent of the problem.

It all adds up to that ruinously expensive project which we call the "space program"—a frenzied attempt by man to find out where his strange visitors come from—and what they want.

3

Is Somebody Up There?

An annual publicity event for the past decade has been the Air Force press release, assuring the public that the Air Force has investigated jillions of flying saucer reports and found nothing to support them. These carefully-contrived releases have deceived many persons but they have not changed the facts one whit. They have only obscured them.

Is there really anything up there? Are there really such things as flying saucers, which the Air Force calls Unidentified Flying Objects?

"YES!" says jet pilot Barry Goldwater, United States Senator. In a written statement to the National Investigations Committee On Aerial Phenomena, Senator Goldwater declares: "Flying saucers—Unidentified Flying Objects—or whatever you call them, are real!"

That view is shared by Vice Admiral R. N. Hillenkoetter, USN Retired, and former head of Central Intelligence, a post that he occupied when the nation's capitol was visited by scores of UFO's in the summer of 1952.

Admiral Delmar S. Fahrney, USNR, former head of the Navy guided missile program, says: "Reliable reports indicate clearly that there are objects coming into our atmosphere at very high speeds. Their maneuvers indicate that they are under intelligent direction."

Captain James Howard, veteran British military and trans-Atlantic pilot, who with crew and passengers saw one huge UFO and six small ones simultaneously: "We are convinced that the things we watched were space craft of design and performance beyond human capabilities."

Astronomers have made public statements on this same subject. The late H. Percy Wilkins, world famous authority on lunar matters, watched a shiny disc-shaped thing maneuver near a plane on which he was a passenger. Said Mr. Wilkins: "I saw a flying saucer. In shape and performance it was unlike anything made by man."

Frank Halstead, for twenty-five years director of the University of Minnesota's Darling Observatory at Duluth, has seen and reported several of these unconventional objects. He said of them: "They were tremendous in size—awesome to behold. Mankind must be prepared to accept the fact that we are having visitors from elsewhere in space."

Clyde Tombaugh, famed astronomer of Lowell Observatory in Flagstaff, with his wife and daughter watched a strange lighted craft maneuver over the desert near their home." In all my years observing the skies I had never seen anything remotely like it. It was controlled, I am sure. I felt that we were watching a space ship."

Astronaut Gordon Cooper took a long chance with the censorship restrictions when he wrote: "*****I don't believe in fairy tales, but, as far as I am concerned, there have been far too many unexplained examples of UFO sightings around this earth for us to rule out the possibility that some form of life exists out there beyond our own world." (Quote is from the book "We Seven" published 1962 by Simon and Schuster.)

Life in space?

If we are willing to accept the presence of the Unidentified Flying Objects which have been seen and studied and photographed all over the world, then it follows that for them to be directed craft there must be some intelligent direction by living beings of some sort—somewhere.

In late 1962 Dr. Carl Sagan, advisor on Extraterrestial Life to the Armed Services of the United States, told the American Rocket Society convention that we must be prepared to face the probability that we have been visited by intelligent beings from outer space—and the likelihood that as a requisite to those visits they would have used bases on the averted side of the moon.

Dr. Harold C. Urey, member of the Mars Committee and world-reknowned nuclear scientist, said in a published statement: "It is exceedingly probable that there is other life in the universe more intelligent than ours."

Dr. Harlow Shapley, former director of Harvard Observatory, made it somewhat more specific than Dr. Urey. Said Shapley: "We must now accept it as inevitable—there are other worlds with thinking beings."

Speaking at Milliken University in Decatur, Illinois, on January 9, 1963, Brigadier General John McDavid, an aide to the Joint Chiefs of Staff, told the audience:

"Before long people will be forced to accept as a fact that this earth is but a grain of sand in an infinite universe —that the human is but one of many forms of life with which God is concerned—and that others are far superior to us."

Strange craft roaming the skies with performance characteristics far beyond those of any man-made device; eminent scientists and military leaders repeatedly referring to the existence of supra-intelligent creatures whom we must expect to contact with unforeseeable results.

In order to believe the Air Force pronouncements that such craft and creatures do not exist, we must dismiss the statements of these eminent world leaders whom we have just quoted as so much nonsense.

Unfortunately for the Air Force protestations, there is ample evidence that they are engaged in a policy of deceiving the public; that they do not believe their own denials nor practice their own preaching.

For example:

The Air Force denies that any Unidentified Flying Objects were over Washington, D. C. on the night of August 13th, 1952.

The Civil Aeronautics Administration produced Technical Development Report #180-CAA which lists all 68 of the UFO's that were over Washington, D. C. on the night of August 13, 1952, shows how they maneuvered on the radar screens and lists the commercial planes and pilots involved in the events of that night.

That the Air Force does not believe that there are no extra-terrestial craft in our skies is clearly shown in an Air Force Intelligence Manual which carries a drawing of a flying saucer for the guidance of personnel involved in the investigations of such things.

And the document that firmly nails the Air Force denials as falsehoods is an order issued by the Director General of the Air Force on December 24, 1959, to all Air Base Commanders. This document is entitled: "UFO's Are Serious Business" and the first sentence says: "Unidentified flying objects—sometimes treated lightly in the press and referred to as "flying saucers"—must be rapidly and accurately identified as serious U. S. Air Force business."

The balance of that document is devoted to telling how the UFO cases must be handled—including a container in which the investigator may collect samples of the object.

If they aren't there in the first place, how can you collect samples of them?

4

The Face on the Wall

Among the unexplained and unexplainable events of our own days, we may have to list the peculiar occurrence which has taken place in The Tabernacle of Glad Tidings, at Nassau, in the Bahamas. It all began without warning on the Sabbath of January 20, 1963, while the Reverend Paul Roberts was preaching his morning sermon. A young housewife, Mrs. Euna Lowe, leaped to her feet and shouted that she could see Christ.

"He is here!" she cried, "He is here!"

The startled congregation turned their gaze to the spot which she indicated on the newly painted church wall. Sorry to say, they saw nothing unusual. But Mrs. Lowe kept insisting that she could see the face of Jesus, along with another she did not recognize . . . and she seemed amazed that the rest of the audience could not see them, too. The word of this strange incident quickly spread around Nassau and the Reverend Roberts found his church jammed for the evening sermon. He also found that Mrs. Lowe was no longer alone in her claim that she saw the faces . . . most of the congregation insisted that they, too, could *clearly* make out *three* faces—the dominant like-

31

ness being that of Christ. Luther Evans, a representative of the CHICAGO DAILY NEWS, hurried to the church and discovered that he, also, could clearly see three faces outlined on the wall . . . one of them that of Buddha, which he said was less distinct than that of Christ. As Evans stepped close to the wall, the likenesses vanished . . . but when he crossed the room again they were clearly recognizable. The painters who recently redecorated the church were questioned but they could shed no light on the mystery. None of them were artists in any sense of the word and they had simply applied the paint with rollers of the type now familiar to everyone. In this case it is interesting, and perhaps important, to note that when Mrs. Lowe first cried out that she could see the faces, *only she* could see them. But a few hours later they were discernible to everyone and so they remained . . . weeks after the event. What brought them into being remains unknown . . . and it may always be so.

5

Prehistoric Fingerprints

The work of archeologists is fascinating, for it is in reality a form of detective work in which they seek to piece together the story of the human race by studying the scattered and broken bits of evidence left through the ages.

Since early men sought shelter in caves, it was only natural that caves should furnish many traces of their passing. The innumerable pictures traced on cave walls with sticks and fingers and torches still remain in many places—some of them surprisingly well done. But from time to time oddities crop up which are likely to remain question marks forever.

Such a case is that of the great cave at Gargas in southern France. There, on what were once the muddy walls of the cavern, the early dwellers pressed their handprints into the soft clay, establishing a prehistoric fingerprint salon of sorts. In the fullness of time the clay hardened and now the prints are preserved in semi-hard stone.

There are two unusual and interesting features about these prints. Many of them are those of men, women, and even very small children, where the hands had been dipped in red or yellow pigment before they were pressed into the soft clay. In others, the hand was held against the clay and the coloring matter was daubed around it to make an outline.

But the gruesome touch which is found in such abundance in the Gargas cave is the fact that in most of the handprints—even those of little children—one or more of the fingers is missing. And in a few of them, the hand shows no fingers at all—just the stubs where the fingers had been!

Why this should be is unknown, even to those who have spent a lifetime studying such matters. But there is the story, frozen in the soft stone of the cavern walls, defying modern man to decipher it after these thousands of years.

6

Ghost Lights

Among the most frequent forms of light phenomena are the so-called "ghost lights" which crop up in the news from time to time. Perhaps the best-known example in the United States is that of the Brown Mountain lights in North Carolina. They have been watched for almost a hundred and fifty years, sometimes at close range. They are described as yellowish, or sometimes pinkish, orbs of light which seem to flit about on the upper half of that mountain. Those who have seen them at close range say they emit a sizzling or frying sound. Some scientists who have watched them have dismissed them as nothing more than reflections of automobile headlights. This fails to explain what they were in the century before the automobile came blinking along.

Hornet, Missouri, is attaining a measure of renown as the location of still another of these ghost lights.

First noted about 1901, the Hornet light is a glowing orange sphere that bobs around in the same general area on summer nights, year after year. The location, in case you're of a mind to go see for yourself, is twelve miles southwest of Joplin or, to be more precise, two miles southwest of the village of Hornet on a gravel road just off Missouri State Road 43.

The Hornet light has been photographed many times and, with modern high-speed films, that is easy to do. The net result is a circular spot of light which doesn't tell much except that it does confirm that you saw *something*.

The light is customarily observed along the same stretch of the same road, about a mile and a quarter west of the Missouri state line. The gravel road at that point runs through a thick growth of scrub oak which closely borders the road. On dark nights it is a spooky place and the light does nothing to detract from that impression.

While the exact nature of its performance varies from night to night, in general it appears suddenly over the road at a height of from four to ten feet. Just a white ball of light about the size of a baseball at first. It sometimes streaks down the road at bullet velocity, changing color to yellow or orange as it moves—only to stop as though it had struck a brick wall. The light seems to be repelled by people or vehicles which approach it and it moves away from them or disappears—only to reappear a moment later hundreds of feet distant.

Since this manifestation is on a gravel road, the inevitable attempt to explain it as automobile headlights was made. This would seem to be as far from the truth as it was in the Brown Mountain case. At Hornet, as recently as 1962, determined persons have *surrounded* the light as it bobbed along the road. Had it been nothing more than a reflection of distant headlights it would have been visible only to those moving directly toward the source. As it was, the elusive light could be seen from all sides when the investigators had a view of the road. In this particular case, it remained over the road until some of the party got to within twenty-five or thirty feet. Then it blinked out, and blinked back on again tantalizingly a few seconds later over a little nearby field.

During World War II, the U.S. Army Engineers sent some men with gear to the scene of the Hornet light. They used telescopes, cameras, surveyors' transits, Geiger counters, and other gear. They tested caves, mineral deposits, and water supplies in the area. They found nothing except the same baffling, bounding, blob of light which has been performing there since the days of the Quapaw Indians. Since the Indians had no automobiles on which to pin the light, they referred to it simply as a spirit light.

Whatever it is, it always was.

Among the strange lights that bob about the country-side to plague the explainers from time to time, we must include the ghostly orb that danced about in the cemetery at Silver Cliff, Colorado. It—or they—was first noticed by a passer-by in April of 1956—a bluish, pulsating ball of light about the size of a basketball. Sometimes there were two of them; and, upon at least one occasion, there were three of the lights visible at the same time.

Ray DeWall, who publishes the WET MOUNTAIN TRIBUNE at Westcliffe, a mile west of Silver Cliff, was among a crowd of the curious numbering about fifty who pursued the lights around in the cemetery one night. Their efforts were futile. As they drew near the lights, the things would simply vanish, only to reappear at another spot some distance away.

Said the WET MOUNTAIN TRIBUNE: "The lights hover about the tops of the tombstones, but at other times they appear to be on the ground or even up to head high."

As mysteriously as they came, the lights went away, taking their secret with them.

To the list of current "ghost lights" we might add those of Gonzales, Louisiana, and of Suffolk County, Virginia.

The Louisiana light was first noticed about April of 1951, along a five-mile stretch of gravel road between Gonzales and Galvez. The Sheriff, Hickley Waguespack, was among the scores who watched the eerie ball of light flitting around the road and over the nearby treetops. As has happened in similar cases, the Gonzales light blinks out when the curious come too close—and reappears seconds later at a distance safe from pursuit.

On March 5, 1951, residents of Suffolk County, Virginia, noticed their strange nighttime visitor—a glowing blob of light that hovered over rural highways about five feet above the ground, especially on what is called the Jackson Road. Old-timers say the light is not new, but was known to them and to their parents before them. The Virginia State Trooper who investigated, Sergeant W. S. Dameron, says the light is so bright that it looks like a locomotive coming down the road; and C. E. Howell, an official of the Norfolk and Western Railway who has also seen the phenomenon, has agreed with the trooper.

Ghost Lights

Motorists who use Highway 90 between Marfa and Alpine, Texas, often witness the so-called "spook light" which centers its activities around a small peak in the Chinati Mountains.

Watchers who have observed the light through powerful binoculars and telescopes say that it generally appears as a mere dot. Then it sometimes swells to a brilliant ball, or at times a double ball, of glowing white light as bright as a locomotive headlight. Ofttimes it blinks out abruptly, but generally it fades and pulsates before disappearing.

The Chinati light has been observed for more than eighty years and it was evidently known to the Indians, who attributed it to the spirit of an Apache chief doomed to roam those mountains forever.

There are the usual "explanations," including swamp gas (on top of a mountain!), uranium deposits (Geiger counters show no uranium on that peak), and moonlight on a mica deposit (on moonless nights?).

This is one of those cases where the explanations are more baffling than the phenomenon.

7

His Alibi Was Death!

When Chicago police undertook to solve the attempted burglary of a plush North Side apartment, they had every reason to believe that the chase would be short and the solution final;—for two witnesses assured police that they had recognized the man who fled from the scene of the crime. The date was April 4, 1953 —and the burglary was attempted at 1:30 on a bright sunshiny afternoon when the witnesses had good visibility. The burglar, they told police, was thirty-two-year-old William Brooks. They said they had seen him fleeing from the building after failing to pry open the door of the apartment.

True or False?

Chicago detectives quickly found Brooks and brought him in. A screwdriver found in his car, hidden in the upholstery, fitted precisely in the marks on the apartment door. And at a bench trial the prosecutor pointed out to the court that Brooks was a parolee and urged that he be sent back to prison for life as an habitual criminal.

For the young prisoner the outlook at this point was bleak. Penniless, with a bad record behind him, Brooks could expect little mercy from the court. Worst of all, there didn't seem to be much that he could do in his own behalf.

Fortunately for him, there was an interruption in the court at that point and he was taken back to his cell to await the conclusion of his trial on the following day. It wasn't much, but it turned out to be all that was needed; for it gave his court-appointed attorney time to check out the amazing story Brooks told him.

When the accused man next appeared in court the attorney told a remarkable story—Brooks could not have committed the crime with which he was charged because he had been legally dead at the time!

Brooks had been in a Veteran's Hospital under treatment for ulcers and, when he left the hospital in March of 1953, his records had been confused with another veteran of the same name who had died there. On the day of the burglary for which he was accused, Brooks had gone to the Veteran's Administration office in downtown Chicago to prove that he was not dead, so he could continue to receive his military disability pay. At 1:44 P.M., while Brooks was still sitting in the VA office, a telegram had been sent to establish his identity—an action which proved that he certainly was not the man at the scene of the burglary miles away, only fourteen minutes before. By proving to the government that he was not dead, William Brooks proved to the court that he was innocent of the burglary.

8

A Curse upon Them?

During the great witch-hunt mania which swept through Europe for more than three centuries, thousands of innocent persons, generally aged women, were tortured and murdered on the pretext that they had brought ill fortune to others by some sorcery. This form of legalized murder led to the slaughter of an estimated six hundred persons each year in Germany alone, according to Dr. Charles Mackay. It also led to the legend of the curse on the rich and powerful family of the Duke of Bedford.

A member of that family was reportedly instrumental in having an old lady burned at the stake, upon the accusation that she had acted as a witch. The evidence was principally that of persons who disliked the old lady personally—with the usual sprinkling of crackpots and questionables. Since her only defense was denial of the preposterous charges—and her only hope of clemency was from the Duke, who refused to lift a finger in her behalf, she went to the burning stake with bitterness in her heart. There, as they lighted the straw about her, she is said to have called down violent death upon the family.

Some of them did indeed die violently, a rather large

proportion of them, it seems. This has been especially true since the inception of the current century.

In 1937 the Duchess of Bedford died of an overdose of sleeping pills. The Duke's mother had learned to fly a plane at the age of sixty-four and was widely known to newspaper readers as The Flying Duchess. When she was seventy-one, she took off for a routine flight and was never seen again.

The Duke's own fate a few years ago falls into the pattern which has so frequently brought to mind the story of the "witch's curse." His prize lovebirds had been pestered for several days by a small hawk. The Duke decided to kill the hawk. An accomplished hunter, he loaded a gun and set forth one morning to await the arrival of the predator. Instead, he was found mysteriously shot to death. The official verdict was that somehow he had fallen and killed himself with his own gun, a very unlikely performance when all factors are considered. But for whatever reason, another violent death had been added to the long list of such tragedies in the family of the Duke of Bedford.

Ironically, the family slogan is:

"What is to be, will be."

Don Antonio Feliz owned eight thousand acres of fine California land which he acquired through a Mexican land grant in 1775. He was a very successful man, one of the wealthiest in California in his time. His years were long but not all of them were happy; for at the time of his death he had no family of his own.

Feliz made no secret of his preference for a niece, Donna

Petranilla, who fully expected to receive a major share of his immense holdings. But the only will which could be found never mentioned her and, since that was all the courts had on which to base an opinion, she was cut off with nothing more than long and costly court proceedings to show for her efforts. Donna Petranilla screamed that she had been cheated, as perhaps she had.

But she did more than that.

She was an old woman at the time of her death in 1863 and she had nursed that bitterness for a good many years. Donna Petranilla pulled herself up on one elbow and aimed her dying blow at Don Antonio Coronel, the man who had inherited the ranch that she had expected to have. Donna screamed that a blight would fall on the lands of the rancho—"the wrath of heaven and the vengeance of hell " was the way she phrased it. With that she fell back and died.

The curse frightened Coronel so badly that he immediately sought to nullify it by transferring title of the rancho to his lawyer. The lawyer paid no heed to such things as the curses of frustrated old women. Instead, he promptly sold the water rights on the entire rancho for a bargain price of eight thousand dollars. While celebrating the sale, he was killed in a drunken fight.

Rancho Feliz then became the property of wealthy Leon Baldwin, who went bankrupt after fire destroyed his crops and a malady decimated his vast herds of cattle. Baldwin found himself destitute.

The wrath of heaven which Donna Petranilla had mentioned in her denunciation became a reality in 1884. A giant cloudburst sent walls of water thundering down the valleys into the Los Angeles River and every building of the original Rancho Feliz was destroyed in the flood.

A major portion of the rancho eventually became what is today Griffith Park—but ill fortune was still dogging its footsteps. A government works project was instituted to clean up the park and on October 3, 1933, fire roared through the brush, trapping twenty-seven WPA workers who lost their lives.

Since that time, tragedy has not plagued the place. Perhaps the 'curse' of Donna Petranilla has run its course.

9

*The Search for the
Hairy Giants*

When one species of creature is pushed out of its accustomed territory by another, the losers generally retreat to wilder and less desirable terrain. That may explain why the thousands of reports of huge, hairy, sub-human creatures around the world always come from the fringes of the wilderness and jungles. Being not-quite-human they would have to take what was left, and that seems to be exactly what they have done.

There are many names for these creatures but the names all mean the same thing in essence—the wild men.

It is unfortunate that in the Himalayas they have become the subject of the white man's ridicule as a result of their being called "abominable snow men." This came about when their tracks were noted as they crossed from one remote valley to another, making their way across a snow field in the process. They do not live in the snow field and the alleged scientists—mostly publicity hounds—who hunt them in the snow, by so doing reveal their own insincerity.

Because the creatures are generally shy and because they customarily confine themselves to their own remote fastnesses, they are seldom seen by white men. Natives of the Malay peninsula are familiar with them, as are the natives of Mongolia and the Siberian forests and, for that matter, the Indians in our own Northwest. But upon occasion white men have seen them, sometimes at very close range. For instance, there is a report by a Soviet scientist, Dr. A. C. Pronin, leader of a hydrological expedition into the Pamir mountains in Tadzik Republic, Central Asia, in the summer of 1957. Dr. Pronin stated that two of the native guides called his attention to a creature that was sunning itself on a rocky ledge across a shallow valley from where the doctor stood. Using his binoculars, Dr. Pronin got a five-minute look at the creature under excellent viewing conditions. He described it in his report as man-like in structure with unusually long arms. Its face was largely covered with hair and its body was entirely covered with hair that was grayish-brown in color. He estimated that it was about seven feet tall when it stood up. Two days later the doctor got another look at the same or a similar creature, which he said could only be described as sub-human. The natives told him that the creatures were harmless to humans and that they subsisted on roots and berries and small rodents which they dug out from under the rocks.

In June of 1958, Reuters news service reported that natives of the south Sumatran village of Pabamulih had captured alive a strange creature resembling some unknown type of near-human. It was described as a female, estimated to be about sixteen or seventeen years of age and completely covered with hair from head to foot. It was known to Sumatrans as a Sindai, and the government of the Netherlands had once offered a reward to anyone who could bring one in alive. When the natives found that the present Sumatran government had not renewed the bounty offer, they took the creature back into the jungle and turned it loose. It reportedly showed no willingness to eat while in captivity and made no effort to defend itself when surrounded by the natives who brought it in.

This specimen was about five feet tall and looked remarkably human, according to the natives who captured it.

Colonel V. S. Karapetyan, attached to the medical service of the Soviet Army in 1941, was stationed at Buinaksk, which is in the Daghestan Mountains. He filed a report on an incident which occurred there in the winter of 1941, when local authorities came to him and invited him to examine a "wild man" they had captured in the nearby mountains.

Colonel Karapetyan says that the creature was male, barefooted, and naked. It was entirely human in shape and was covered with dark brown hair of shaggy texture on the chest, shoulders, and back. The face, palms, and soles of the feet were not hairy. The sparse hair around the creature's mouth was bristly, similar to a man's beard. The hair on its head was long, very dark brown, and it hung down to the shoulders. It gave the appearance of a man slightly more than six feet tall, broad-shouldered, long-armed, deep-chested. The natives who were caring for the creature told the Colonel that they could not keep their prisoner in a warm house because he perspired so freely that the stench was overpowering.

The Colonel's official report says that the wild man stood before him like a hairy giant—chest out, shoulders squared, huge hands with thick strong fingers hanging almost to his knees.

When offered food, the captive made no response of any kind. He did not fight nor did he make any attempt to talk, other than to whimper softly a time or two.

Says Colonel Karapetyan's report:

"His eyes told me nothing. They were large and dark and they were also dull and empty of expression. They were the eyes of an animal and nothing more."

What became of the creature is not known; for Colonel Karapetyan was transferred from that point a few weeks later, and what must have been one of the most interesting captives on record was lost to science.

In 1939, when Mongolian and Chinese troops were fighting in one of their innumerable border wars, a small party of Mongolian soldiers came upon three strange humanlike creatures scrambling up a hillside. They shot them and reported that the creatures looked like wild men without clothes, covered with hair about three inches long. And that description fits the manlike creature that a Mongolian chemist encountered on a field trip in 1947. He was sitting beside some boulders eating his lunch when he noticed that a hairy manlike creature had come out of a crack in the rocks and was digging around in the soil, evidently searching for food of some sort. The chemist watched the creature for about fifteen minutes from a distance of less than a hundred feet, and his description is similar to that which Colonel Karapetyan gave of the captured wild man he examined.

The natives in the mountainous regions of the American Northwest, from northern California to British Columbia, lived in fear of giant hairy men who assertedly made their home in the dense forests in that area. When the Indians told the white men about these monsters, whom they called the Sasquatch, the white men generally regarded the whole business as another piece of primitive fiction.

But as time went on, and some of the white men themselves came out of those same mountains with their own experiences to recount, the Indians' stories began to seem more credible.

When the Victoria, B. C., DAILY BRITISH COLONIST made its remarkable report from Yale, British Columbia, under date of July 3, 1884, a lot of people who had stories to tell of these Sasquatch began to step forward. The DAILY BRITISH COLONIST told how a train crew had spotted a creature that appeared to be half man and half ape lying beside the tracks at a deep cut about twenty miles north of Yale. The train was hurriedly stopped, and the train crew managed to grab the creature as it attempted to scale the steep rocky bank. Unable to take it alive without being scratched or bitten, one of the trainmen got above it and knocked it senseless with a piece of stone. They tied the creature with a bell rope and put it in the baggage car. A large crowd assembled to see the captive when the train reached its destination.

The paper quotes the train crew as speculating that Jacko, as they called their captive, had ventured too close to the edge of the cut and had fallen to the track, stunning himself, which might explain why he was lying in the open when first seen.

Within a day or two, he was fully recovered and none the worse for his rough treatment. He looked like a small hairy man covered with black silky hair except for the hands, feet, and face. He walked on two feet, was about four feet ten inches tall, and weighed 127 pounds.

Unfortunately, Jacko was allowed to leave the scene with some itinerant showman and what befell him is unknown. But from the description it seems likely that he was a young specimen of the Sasquatch—and that as he grew to maturity his fur would have changed color.

Mr. and Mrs. George Chapman and their three small children lived in a cabin near the little town of Ruby Creek on the Frazer River in the summer of 1941, which places them about twenty-two miles south of the spot where Jacko had been captured by the train crew back in 1884. Chapman worked for the railroad, and his journeys left his youngsters, a nine-year-old boy and two younger children, to be cared for by the mother.

The eldest boy ran into the house to tell his mother that some big animal was moving around in the bushes behind the field in back of the house. Mrs. Chapman took a look and decided that it was a bear—but she was soon disabused of that idea, for the creature burst out of the bushes into full view and she saw a giant hairy manlike thing, walking slowly toward her and the children. While the children fled toward the river, she followed slowly behind them, between them and the Sasquatch. She could clearly see that it was covered with shaggy fur or hair, that it walked erect, and that its face was human or nearly so.

While the mother and three children were fleeing down the river bank, the intruder (as they discovered after Mr. Chapman got home) was busy rummaging through the house and terminated his visit by tearing open a keg of salt fish which he scattered around the yard.

Mrs. Chapman estimated the creature's height at seven and a half or eight feet—and its giant footprints in the mud around the house were like those of a huge barefoot man with second toes longer than the great toe. Brownish hairs caught in the door jamb confirmed Mrs. Chapman's guess that the thing was at least seven and one-half feet tall.

The Chapmans, incidentally, moved closer to town shortly after this incident.

The vast wilderness areas of the northwestern United States have been the scene of hundreds of encounters between modern man and these half-men or hairy giants known as Sasquatch. In 1924 a gang of loggers (pretty hairy citizens themselves!) left their camp in the forest and refused to go back because they had been besieged by several giant apelike creatures that pelted the loggers with rocks and clubs and tore up the camp.

And in August of 1958, when a road-building crew was driving a road into the mountain wilderness near Bluff Creek, in Humboldt County, California, they were surprised one morning to find what appeared to be giant human footprints around the equipment, clearly defined in the fine dust. The same thing happened for several days and then things became more interesting. The owner of those sixteen-inch bare feet with the fifty-inch stride picked up a seven-hundred-pound tire and wheel for a bulldozer and carried it several hundred yards before dropping it. And a steel drum of oil weighing three hundred pounds was carried up a steep mountainside and finally tossed into a deep and rocky ravine. Because of the size and weight, it took several men to handle it; but Big Foot, as that particular Sasquatch became known, carried it with no assistance and apparently without strain.

Before the giant transferred his nightly probes to some more remote area, plaster casts were made of his footprints and they confirmed the descriptions the road crew had given of a manlike foot, seventeen inches long and eight inches across the ball of the foot. And this one also displays the anatomical peculiarity that has been noted elsewhere—the second toe is longer than the great toe.

Robert Hatfield is a logger who lived in Crescent City, California, in February of 1962; but at the time of this incident he was visiting with some friends, Mr. and Mrs. Bud Jenkins, who lived four miles from Fort Bragg, California. Hatfield heard the Jenkins' dog howling in terror and he went out to see what was bothering the hound.

He found out quickly enough.

At the back of the yard, about sixty feet from where Hatfield was standing, a huge hairy monster with a near-human face was peering at him over a fence. Since the fence was six feet high and since this creature's chest and head were above the fence, it was unquestionably more than seven feet tall.

At first Hatfield thought he was looking at an immense bear—the biggest bear he had ever seen. He ran into the house and roused Jenkins to come and see it too. A few moments later when both men hurried back outside, neither of them saw it at first. Hatfield dashed around the corner of the house and ran into the creature, knocking himself sprawling in the process. Hatfield yelled for the Jenkinses to get into the house—"it's half man and half beast!"

Hatfield scrambled to his feet and raced for the door again, the "thing" right on his heels. He got in, but the creature kept snuffing and pushing on the door to such an extent that the two men's combined efforts could not shut it.

When the pressure eased off for a moment, Jenkins ran to get a rifle. By the time he loaded the weapon and returned with it, the creature was gone and they had only the huge footprints to support their story—the footprints —and a muddy handprint on the side of the white house. This handprint, eleven inches across, was photographed, and casts were made of the footprints, which showed one toe missing.

Hatfield told newsmen he would never forget the face that looked down at him as he lay sprawled on the ground. A nearly black face with stubbly bristles around the mouth and cheeks, and large black eyes; almost, but not quite, human.

The story of the Sasquatch is by no means complete, for it remains for someone to bring one in for examination by qualified experts. The evidence indicating that some sort of humanoid creatures exist in the wilderness areas of the Northwest is voluminous. In fact, it is a logical place for such creatures to dwell, if they exist at all, for in our own mountainous West and Northwest there are tens of thousand of square miles which are still un-mapped and where few, if any, men have ever set foot.

There seems little question that Big Foot and his family are in there. How to get him out, preferably alive, is the next question.

10

UFO Explodes Over Nevada

If the night skies of the United States were invaded by an unidentified craft—if that craft were to be tracked by radar across a dozen states—and if that craft or a similar one were to land beside an electric power station and put it out of operation for forty minutes—that should certainly constitute front page news from coast to coast. And if that same object or craft then took off, pursued by armed jet interceptors which chased it until it exploded in the air over the continental United States, that should certainly be one of the big stories of the year.

ALL THESE THINGS HAPPENED ON THE NIGHT OF APRIL 18, 1962, AND WERE CONFIRMED BY OFFICIAL SPOKESMEN FOR THE STRATEGIC AIR COMMAND AND THE U.S. AIR FORCE—BUT THE STORY WAS SUPPRESSED ON— OR BY—THE NEWS SERVICES!

Fortunately, the Las Vegas (Nevada) Sun checked the story and gave it the front page banner headlines it deserved.

Here is the full, incredible story, which most of the American public never heard of, either because the news services did not make it available—or because their local newspapers, brainwashed by Air Force propaganda, were unwilling to print it.

About 7:30 P.M. on the night of April 18, 1962, something exploded over southwestern Nevada. It shook the earth. It was as brilliant as an atomic blast—which it may have been. The roar made the earth tremble for miles around.

What was it?

The LAS VEGAS SUN went right to work on that aspect of this remarkable incident.

Was it just another of the strange objects which would be explained away as nothing more than a meteorite, meeting its fiery doom as it thundered into the atmosphere?

The reporter who called Nellis Air Force Base evidently took them by surprise, for he was told:

"There's only one thing wrong with that (the meteor supposition)—a meteor cannot be tracked on radar and this thing was!"

Tracked on radar? That's what the spokesman at Nellis Air Force Base said! How much radar tracking had been done on this strange glowing object before it exploded over the Mesquite Range in Nevada?

The logical place to make that inquiry was of the North American Air Defense Command Center at Colorado Springs, Colorado, the nerve center for aerial protection of the continental United States. The spokesman there on the memorable night of April 18, 1962, was Lieutenant

Author's Note: Ionized trails of meteors but not the meteors themselves can be tracked by radar.

57

Colonel Herbert Rolph. He told newsmen that the Air Defense Command had been alerted by the fire trail of this strange object. The first report had come from Oneida, New York, where watchers had detected a glowing red object moving deeper into the United States and apparently at great altitude.

Was it a meteor . . . a missile . . . an enemy aircraft . . . ?

Radar picked it up—so it could not have been a meteor.

A missile? It was traveling too slowly to be a missile.

An enemy aircraft?

Not at that altitude, where even our rocket-powered X-15 could not fly more than a few minutes.

Technically, then, this was an unidentified flying object which had to be kept under close surveillance, if possible. It may be pure coincidence, of course, but "Unidentified Flying Object"—or UFO—is the Air Force's official name for the so-called "flying saucers."

As the intruder penetrated deeper into the Midwest, the Air Defense Command admittedly alerted its bases (including Nellis Air Force Base), and jet interceptors had been hurriedly scrambled from Phoenix to intercept, if possible, the disconcerting and possibly dangerous aerial intruder.

This official admission from the Air Defense Command emphasizes that the object under pursuit was not a meteor. Reports poured in as the thing sped westward: from Oneida, New York, then from Gridley, Kansas, and then from Utah, Montana, New Mexico, Wyoming, Arizona, and California.

In Nephi, Utah, about ninety miles west of Salt Lake City, observers said the glowing red thing passed directly overhead on a horizontal course from east to west. Rumbling sounds were heard by many. If the jets had reached the path of the intruder they were evidently blacked out, for none of the witnesses reported seeing any planes. This does not rule out the possibility that the jets were there, however; for it was quite dark and their passage might have produced the strange rumblings that were reported.

The Air Defense Command said that the object under pursuit vanished from its radar screens at a point about seventy miles northwest of Las Vegas, which coincided with the location of the brilliant explosion that took place somewhere above the Mesquite Range, in the desolate area south of Reno. The flash was so bright that the streets of Reno were lighted as though by a gigantic photographic flash bulb. The flash was also seen at points in California by witnesses who presumed that it was an atomic air test shot over Nevada. However, that was ruled out when the Atomic Energy Commission flatly declared that there were no nuclear tests under way anywhere on the North American continent, airborne or otherwise.

Thus far the story was the official admission that some kind of red, glowing, Unidentified Flying Object had been tracked from New York to Nevada by radar and that armed jet interceptors were after it when the thing vanished from the radar screens following a brilliant and terrifically violent aerial explosion over western Nevada.

The second chapter to this interesting and important story came to light a few hours later, when the United Press news service informed some of its subscribers that a huge object of unknown identity had landed near an electric power station at Eureka, Utah.

The LAS VEGAS SUN went right back to work by renewing their questioning of the Air Force spokesmen, some of whom were showing a reluctance to discuss the matter further. But the spokesman at Stead Air Force Base in Reno admitted that the UP story about the landing was correct. The spokesman declined to say what the nature of the object had been, but he did admit that the landing had taken place and that the electric power station had been put out of operation by what he called the "impact" of the thing. He also admitted that news of this incident had been withheld until the power station had been restored to service.

An unidentified object crossed most of the United States that night. An unidentified object landed beside an electric power station at Eureka, Utah, and the station was out of operation for more than half an hour. The nature of the object which landed with such alleged "impact" was not revealed—because the object did not remain there. The jets were pursuing an unidentified object over southwestern Nevada—after the Eureka incident—when the object exploded in a blinding flash which resembled an atomic explosion.

A fascinating story—an important story—but, outside of the readers of the LAS VEGAS SUN and a few other regional papers, the American public never heard of it.

All the "news management" is not done by the government.

There are times, it seems, when the news agencies themselves miss out on stories such as this one—either because they were not furnished with the material—or because they were unwilling to carry it if they got it.

11

Disasters for the Birds

In mid-October of the year 1846, some sections of France were subjected to the phenomenon of red rain, mixed with birds, dead or half-dead. *Comptes Rendus,* Volumes 23 and 24, contains the details of this unique celestial broth. Just what the red coloring consisted of is not clear from the deliberations of the scientists who were forced to deal with this event. There was no such problem regarding the birds which came tumbling down with the thick red rain, however. Hundreds, perhaps thousands, of battered and bedraggled quail, larks, robins, ducks and water hens came tumbling down. Most of them were presumed to have been dead when they struck; a few were able to effect glancing approaches which prolonged their lives for a few hours. It was, as the scientists of Lyons and Grenoble concluded after surveying the evidence, a most unusual occurrence.

Nor was it without parallel. In July of 1896 the sky over Baton Rouge, Louisiana, divested itself of a sizable collection of defunct birds. On a clear day the startled citizens of Baton Rouge were pelted with dead woodpeckers, catbirds, thrushes, blackbirds, and a few wild ducks; and interested parties noted among the hundreds of specimens numerous birds that were unknown to them and some that were quite rare, which appeared to be canaries.

Against this background, let us now consider the experience which befell a city policeman in Capitola, California, one warm night in August of 1960.

Officer Ed Cunningham was driving along in the patrol car on a routine trip through the city streets, shortly past 2:30 in the morning.

Something flashed in the headlights of the car. Whatever it was, it fell into the street about a hundred feet ahead of him, and bounced a few inches. Was someone throwing something at him? Before he could decide, a second object—a third—a fourth—came tumbling down. Then the officer saw that the things were birds—dead birds, and sizable ones at that. He started to get out of his car to investigate this remarkable deluge—and then changed his mind.

Said Officer Cunningham: "By the time I had stopped the car they were raining down all around me. They were big birds and they were falling so fast and hard they would have knocked me senseless. I thought I had better stay in the car and that's just what I did!"

When circumstances permitted, the officer drove from Capitola to Cliffside and then on to West Cliff Drive, a distance of about five miles around the shore highway. He found the highway and the beach and the roadside littered with dead birds.

Next morning the citizens of the affected communities were treated to the strange spectacle of power lines festooned with birds. Others were impaled on television antennas, fence posts, and jammed into shrubbery by the force of their falls. The birds were identified as Sooty Shearings, a kind of petrel that achieves a wing spread of more than thirty inches and a body length of as much as a foot and a half. They roam the Pacific, making the swing from their nesting grounds in the Australian area around the coastlines of Japan, the Aleutians, and down the west coast of the Americas.

Authorities estimated that about four thousand of the big birds were killed outright around Capitola and another two thousand survived the plunge but could not get off the ground. When kindhearted citizens lugged the ailing birds back to the sea, however, the gulls generally managed to recover sufficiently to fly away.

There were numerous theories which sought to explain the strange deluge of Sooty Shearings. Bad food, dazzled by city lights, and some rare but unspecified bird disease were among the suggestions. Examination of the dead birds failed to confirm any of these hypotheses. The experts could only agree that the big birds had been killed by the fall. Why they fell remains a mystery.

12

With Half a Brain

Let's call the little girl Marie, which is not her real name. Because of the nature of her ailment and of the treatment she underwent, the hospital did not want to reveal her identity. Here is her strange story, taken from the hospital records.

When Marie was one year old she contracted the disease known as sleeping sickness. For weeks she hovered between life and death and, when she finally passed the critical point, it was found that one side of her body was partially paralyzed. Furthermore, this sweet little blue-eyed one-year-old blonde girl had undergone a drastic personality change. Where she had formerly been playful and happy she became morose and sullen. She screamed and tore up her toys, when she could lay hands upon them. And to make matters worse she began having convulsions, from ten to twenty of them each day. It was apparent to the doctors on the case that this unfortunate child was headed for an institution. Then they held a consultation, and decided that there was a chance . . . just one long chance, for little Marie to win her battle with the damaged brain.

She was taken back to Wesley Hospital in Chicago when she was able to make the trip. Since it seemed that one-half of her brain was entirely responsible for her condition —for both the bad behavior and the seizures—the doctors decided that surgery on that area might help her—if she survived. The operation lasted four hours and thirty-five minutes. On May 14, 1951, they removed the right half of her brain. The results exceeded the doctors' fondest hopes. Within three weeks little Marie was showing unmistakable improvement. The hospital disclosed that the remaining half of the child's brain had taken over all functions. Her senses remained acute. The convulsions ended. She was still paralyzed on the left side, but even that condition was showing signs of improvement. And perhaps most remarkable, the recalcitrant, moody child of a few months past became a happy playful girl once again. Five years after the operation, she was still on the mend—a modern scientific miracle.

13

Phoney Quotes

A source of great annoyance to many famous persons is that of being quoted in statements which they did not make . . . and did not want to make.

General Cambronne, the testy little cohort of Napoleon, is often quoted as saying: "The Old Guard dies—but it never surrenders." It is a brave statement and it is attributed to him at the Battle of Waterloo, when the remnant of his army was gathered about him, facing annihilation.

There is only one thing wrong with the story. *General Cambronne never said it.* He spent the rest of his life *denying* that he said it—or that he *could* have said it. But that aggravating misquotation followed him to the grave —where it is carved on his headstone. As he pointed out so many times, it would have been ridiculous for him to have said that "the Old Guard dies but never surrenders" . . . for the *Old Guard did not die at all . . . it surrendered!*

In more recent times we have the classic experience of the leader of the United States forces in Europe during the first World War—General John J. Pershing. Thousands of publications carried his picture, standing before the tomb of Lafayette in Paris. The caption quoted Pershing as saying "Lafayette, we are here!" It is a great line, an historic line—but Pershing not only never said it . . . it never even occurred to him. In 1931 he wrote a book about his life in which he said: "It has been mistakenly reported that I stood before the tomb of Lafayette in Paris on July 4, 1917, and said, 'Lafayette, we are here!' It is such a striking utterance that I wish I might have said it—but I did not. The credit must go to my good friend, Colonel Stanhope." But the Colonel was forgotten and the misquotation followed Pershing to the grave . . . and into the history books.

Another famous example is the line attributed to Voltaire and long carried at the masthead of many newspapers, including the NEW YORK HERALD TRIBUNE: "I disapprove of what you say but I will defend to the death your right to say it." Students of Voltaire finally traced it to Evelyn Hall, who admitted Voltaire had not said it . . . but that she had quoted him as saying it because "it sounded so much like him!"

14

The Home
With the Hum

Rotterdam, New York, is one of the suburbs of Schenectady. It is also the home of a family that lived in a madhouse for months . . . for the family of Eugene Binkowski was bedeviled by a hum that wouldn't quit during at least nine consecutive months. Mr. Binkowski is a truck driver and by no means a neurotic. First signs of trouble were headaches, toothaches, earaches, and stiffening of the joints for the various members of the family.

Then they began to realize that day and night they were bathed in a faint humming sound that never stopped. They reported to police, who were properly baffled. It was inevitable that the nearby General Electric plant should become interested, and its technicians investigated. They professed to hear no sound of an unusual nature and admitted that they had no idea what caused the ailments that were plaguing the family.

In desperation Mr. Binkowski wrote to President Kennedy and sought help. A few days later a group of six Air Force sound experts arrived, along with considerable delicate gear designed to detect high-frequency sound. In spite of half-a-million dollars' worth of gear, they were unable to trace any sounds which might be causing the family's trouble. They did discover, however, that the entire family seemed to possess unusually acute hearing. Six-year-old Terry Binkowski, for example, could detect sounds up to 21,000 cycles per second, well above the normal hearing range. The Air Force experts left with the mystery unsolved—telling the family that their troubles might be based on three nearby radio stations . . . but how or why was left unexplained.

Hundreds of persons visited the Binkowski house out of curiosity—and most of them either heard the hum—or felt a stuffiness they could not account for. The Air Force techicians confirmed that the family was physically capable i hearing what it claimed to hear. Beyond that, there have Jeen no explanations of the annoying hum . . . and the Binkowskis decided to move into a nearby garage . . . in the hope the hum would go away.

15

Treasure from the Bible

In recent years scientific researchers have been surprised—sometimes pleasantly—by the results they have secured through literal translation and study of the Bible.

In the water-starved Holy Land, any dependable source of supply deserved mention, and the ancient pool of Gibeon was mentioned in the Bible. Tracing out the reference, Dr. James Pritchard of the University of Pennsylvania Museum led a group which found the pool, only eight miles north of Jerusalem.

Ancient engineers had painstakingly dug a pit thirty-seven feet in diameter and thirty-five feet down in the hard limestone; at that point they had carved a stairway into the face of the pit and offset a tunnel down to the eighty-two-foot level where they found pure water and plenty of it—the water that was used in the flourishing wine production of Gibeon.

When the armies of Nebuchadnezzar overran the country in 587 B.C., one of their first acts was to destroy, wherever possible, the natural resources of the conquered. In keeping with this policy, they dumped hundreds of tons of stone and dirt into the great well; and time finished the job by sealing it up and erasing it from the memories of men. But the Bible did not forget; it furnished the clues which led the University of Pennsylvania scientists to the site, and today the pool of Gibeon flows again, after being lost for twenty-five hundred years.

In the eighth chapter and ninth verse of Deuteronomy it says: "For the Lord thy God bringeth thee into a good land . . . whose stones are iron and out of whose hills thou canst dig copper."

Dr. Nelson Glueck, president of Hebrew Union College, studied that passage and decided that if the Bible were historically accurate, as other cases had indicated, then a search for the lost copper mines might be worthwhile. He was treading on debatable ground; for many eminent scientists of the current scene had expressed the conviction that Solomon had never mined copper.

Dr. Glueck noted that the Bible said that Solomon's ships were sent to trade with the Persian kings and the vessels returned laden with gold and spices. What did they trade for those cargoes? Was it copper? Assuming that copper was one of Solomon's major exports, Dr. Glueck began the search for the port of Ezion Geber on the Gulf of Aqabah, said to have been a flourishing spot in Solomon's days.

His detective work, actually a fine piece of archeological research, located and identified the long lost port. There remained only the task of locating the mines themselves—if indeed such mines ever existd.

Color photographs taken from high flying planes furnished the first hints that there might be copper in certain of those barren, windswept ridges. Intensive search by ground parties began to produce evidence of long abandoned water holes in certain areas. Patiently assembling the evidence that men had shown prolonged and unusual interest in two of the ridges, Dr. Glueck and his crew finally reduced their studies to just one stony rift, known now as Wadi el Arabah. There they found ancient mines—and the scattered remains of the·little smelters which had used the water from the ancient water holes. There they also found veins of copper still unworked, sometimes with the crumbling picks lying along the tunnels where the workmen had dropped them, to flee from the invaders thousands of years ago.

Those mines are back in production today; for in 1957 Dr. Glueck discovered that it is still true, as Deuteronomy had said, "out of those hills thou canst dig copper."

Although the Dead Sea Scrolls mention sixty separate hoards of treasure—all of them within fifty miles of the Dead Sea—time has obliterated many of the landmarks and erosion has changed others almost, if not quite, beyond recognition.

The obscure sect which produced the scrolls and secreted the treasure evidently placed great importance on the portion of the scrolls dealing with this subject; for they painstakingly punched the information into thin sheets of copper—a laborious and costly process for them. But their efforts were not in vain, for their message is 95 per cent intelligible after two thousand years.

The scrolls describe the hiding places of an estimated

72

two hundred tons of gold, largely in bars—a treasure which would be worth more than two hundred million dollars today . . . if it could be found.

One tantalizing inscription reads:

"In the cistern, which is below the rampart, on the east side in a place hollowed out of the rock, there will be found 600 large bars of silver. Close by, under the southern corner of Zadok's tomb, and underneath a column of pilaster in the exedras, there is a golden vessel of incense in pine wood and another vessel in cassia wood. In the pit nearby, toward the north and near to the grave, in a hole opening to the north, there is a copy of this book with explanations, measurements, and all details."

Scientists know that the Zadok mentioned in this fascinating treasure map was in reality a high priest of King Solomon. Scholars also believe that they know the location of his tomb, for Zadok's burial is referred to in several ancient writings.

With the aid of modern electronic gear, they may be able to find that particular treasure trove—and the book of measurements and instructions—if they are still there after all these centuries.

16

Castle with a Curse

If it is possible for a building to be cursed, then Miramar Castle is such a place. It stands lovely and aloof along the edge of the blue Adriatic near Trieste—and many who are familiar with the palace and its story believe that it is the scene of a curse. The evidence? Here is the story of Miramar Castle . . .

It was built about the middle of the nineteenth century by Emperor Franz Joseph of Austria as a present for his brother, the Archduke Maximilian. The Archduke had lived in Miramar only a few years when he left it to become the Emperor of Mexico, an adventure that led to his death before a firing squad.

Next to reside in the ill-starred castle were Maximilian's sister-in-law, Empress Elizabeth of Austria, and her son, Rudolph, the heir to the Austrian throne. In 1889 Rudolph and his mistress were found shot to death at Mayerling, near Vienna. Nine years later Empress Elizabeth was stabbed to death in Geneva.

Already rumors of the curse on Miramar Castle had been whispered about. Archduke Francis Ferdinand, Rudolph's cousin and next in line for the throne, laughed at what he called the silly superstition about the castle . . .

and moved in. He, too, paid with his life . . . for he and his wife were shot to death in the streets of Sarajevo—the spark that touched off the first World War.

Maximilian, Rudolph, Elizabeth, then Francis Ferdinand and his wife . . . all residents of the so-called accursed castle . . . and all victims of violence. Who would be next?

After World War I ended, Trieste and the castle both became the property of Italy as part of the spoils of war. The Duke of Aosta got his wish . . . he moved into Miramar Castle and for a time the future looked bright. He sponsored Mussolini, was made Viceroy of Ethiopia . . . only to die miserably as a prisoner of war in British East Africa.

After World War II, American forces took over Trieste for a time and the castle became the temporary home for Major General Bryant Moore and Major General Bernice McFadden. Both of them died of heart attacks.

Some people still believe that Miramar Castle *did* have a curse on it, after all.

17

Monster on the Beach

Although scores of scientists studied the evidence for two years or more, they were never able to identify the thing that was found on the beach.

It is presumed that the creature washed ashore about the middle of July, 1960, when Tasmania underwent one of the worst storms in its history. After the fury of the gales had subsided, rancher Ben Fenton and several of his men were rounding up cattle near a beach about two miles from the point where Interview River empties into the sea. Two of the drovers came upon a huge, fur-covered mass of something lying on the beach, and they reported it to Mr. Fenton. He came and observed and marveled . . . and reported it to the authorities.

After a government naturalist viewed the great lump, other scientists rushed to the scene, some of them by helicopter, to expedite their arrival at this lonely spot.

They found the remains of a gigantic creature unknown in the record books. It was roughly circular in shape, perhaps twenty feet in diameter and six feet thick at the center. It consisted of a fibrous white substance covered with short, bristly brown hair and protected by an inch-thick skin so tough that axes made little impression. In order to hack out a segment for laboratory purposes, two husky scientists chopped at the thing with sharp axes for more than an hour.

Scientific study merely deepened the mystery, for there was no trace of any similar substance or creature in the annals of science. Noted zoologists examined the evidence and declared that it was positively not part of any whale. Other scientists came and saw and declared that it was not part of any known creature. When questions were asked about the monster on the beach in the Australian Parliament in March of 1962, a hastily assembled team of government scientists was flown to the Tasmanian beach to settle the mystery. They announced that they would remain on the site for weeks.

As a matter of fact they were there only twenty-four hours. Their official statement said that it was a gigantic creature . . . but they could only agree that it was unlike anything ever seen before. A year later, the monster on the beach in Tasmania was still there, still unidentified.

18

Ramu the "Wolf Boy"

In reporting to you from time to time on the countless unexplained and unexplainable events which defy science, it also becomes my duty to report to you on the occasional frauds which slip into those same categories.

Thanks to careless or stupid journalism, there crop up from time to time stories of strange children with incredible attributes. Many of you will remember the so-called "Gazelle Boy" of 1951, described in the newspapers as a wild boy who had been found living with gazelles in the sandy wastelands of the Middle East. Upon investigation by competent parties, the "Gazelle Boy" proved to be a mentally retarded child of about thirteen who had strayed away from his nomadic family. His widely advertised fleetness proved to be as nonexistent as his widely reported life among the gazelles.

There died recently in Lucknow, India, a hapless lad known as "Ramu, the Wolf Boy." His official history began when workmen found him huddled in the corner of a railway car one morning in 1954. He was naked, filthy, and could neither speak nor write, a combination of conditions which may also be true of wolves. Perhaps this explains why it was assumed that he had been raised by wolves who thoughtfully put him in that railway car when he outgrew them.

Ramu ofttimes refused to eat the food that was placed before him, and scientists carefully noted that he fought when he was required to take a bath. Unless my memory fails me, these same responses are also characteristic of many children who were not raised by wolves.

Ramu continued to resist the treatment offered by the hospital authorities who tried to convert him to what is known as civilization, and at the time of his death he was still resisting. He was just what he was and he had no desire to be anything else.

Ramu has become the latest in a series of abandoned children whom the excited reporters in India have foisted on the world as "wolf children." Without exception they have all been mentally retarded youngsters whose connection with wolves existed only in the fevered imaginations of irresponsible reporters.

19

Rendezvous with a Light

Maryland State Trooper Bob Burkhardt drove on through the town of Hebron and swung off on a short cut which would take him and the Sergeant beside him back to the main highway. It had been a dull, uneventful evening, the sort that makes police officers wary; for they always suspect the calm before the storm.

Jogging along on the side road at about twenty minutes until midnight, Burkhardt spotted a dim yellow light in the center of the highway a couple of hundred yards ahead. He slowed down quickly; for this narrow country lane was a poor place to encounter some farmer with a lantern hanging on the back of a wagon. In seconds the light was only yards away. The trooper slammed on the brakes and slid to a halt in a cloud of sandy dust.

When the dust settled, the two troopers realized that the light was hovering, not more than twenty feet from their car, right in the glare of the headlights—just sitting there in mid air about five feet off the ground as though awaiting their next move. There was no wagon, no truck, nothing—just that glowing yellow ball of light.

Burkhardt started his engine again and pulled back onto

the road. The light zipped away from the car—a couple of hundred feet in a fraction of a second—then it stopped again. The troopers shot quick glances at each other. Burkhardt's partner drew his gun and rolled down his window. The car sped forward with lights on bright. The ball of light again bounded away from them. No matter how the troopers varied the speed of their car, the light easily maintained the same distance from them. Presently it just blinked out, and the shaken troopers sped off down the highway.

Fearing ridicule, they made no official report that night on this phase of their experiences. But they quietly alerted some of their fellow officers and Burkhardt, along with five off-duty troopers, went to the same area the following night. They found the light waiting for them.

On foot, the men separated and then moved in on the thing, which all of them could see as it hovered over the road. When the ring of men had closed to within fifteen or twenty feet of the glowing ball, it blinked out. A minute later it lit up again in a nearby field, as alert and elusive as ever.

The road, now known as Church Street, Extended, has been the scene of this unusual phenomenon for more than seventy years, according to residents. Hundreds of persons have seen the light, especially since the story of the troopers' experience was published by the Salisbury, Maryland, newspaper in July of 1952. The stock attempt to dismiss the light as nothing more than automobile headlight reflections as usual fails to account for the fact that the light was there long before the automobiles.

20

The Runaway Coffin Comes Home

One of the strangest stories I ever dealt with is also one of the best documented. It is the story of the life and death of Charles Coghlan, who was born on Prince Edward Island, off the east coast of Canada, in 1841. He came from a poor Irish family and when he was ready for school the neighbors donated funds to send Charles to England. He eventually graduated with honors and, to the dismay of his family, announced that he was going to be an actor.

The Coghlans were noted for the firmness of their decisions and Charles was no exception. When his parents informed him that he would be banned from the old homestead unless he gave up his theatrical ambitions, Charles—a true Coghlan himself—reaffirmed his plans for making a career on the stage. It was a brilliant career in which he generally played himself, a sharp-tongued, acerbic fellow of considerable satirical wit. [As an understudy he had a young fellow named Monty Woolley, who later mimicked Coghlan's mannerisms with great success in the movies.]

Coghlan once visited a Gypsy fortune teller who told

him that he would die at the height of his fame in an American southern city, but that he would have no rest until he returned to the place of his birth, Prince Edward Island. Coghlan often mentioned this strange prediction to his friends, evidently because it had made a deep impression on him.

In 1898, while he was playing Hamlet in Galveston, Texas, he died suddenly, and was buried in a Galveston cemetery.

Two years later the great hurricane that swept over that hapless city washed away the sandy cemetery where Coghlan had been buried. Although his family offered a sizable reward, his coffin could not be found.

In October, 1908, eight years and one month after the Galveston hurricane, some fishermen on Prince Edward Island found a huge box, covered with moss and barnacles, floating in the shallows. It contained the coffin and body of Charles Coghlan, including the silver plate which identified him. He had come home at last to the little island three thousand miles from where he had been buried, just as the Gypsy fortune teller had predicted so many years before. Charles Coghlan—brought home by the sea—was finally buried in the cemetery beside the church where he had been baptized sixty-seven years before—one of the strangest true stories on record.

21

UFO over Hawaii

When the so-called "flying saucers" were first noted in sizable numbers, back in 1947, their appearances seemed to follow no given pattern. Later, however, studies showed that they were systematically visiting important military bases, industrial centers, and communications centers. The same studies showed that the strange objects, officially known as Unidentified Flying Objects or UFO's, appeared most frequently in the spring and summer in the Northern Hemisphere, and in the balance of the year went to the southern half of the globe when warm weather moved to that area.

In the years of 1960, 1961, and 1962, the strange objects appeared with predictable regularity at the time of satellite launchings. They were on hand when we conducted hydrogen bomb tests in the Pacific in 1962. A group of objects moving in formation followed Captain Joe Walker as he made a test flight in the rocket plane X-15, traveling at several thousand miles an hour high above the atmosphere. Walker's wing cameras photographed the formation and, although the public was told that the things which followed his plane were only gigantic "ice flakes," officials flatly refused to let the public see the films.

UFO Over Hawaii

About 8 p.m. on the night of March 11, 1963, a glowing circular object was sighted high in the heavens over Hawaii. Hundreds, perhaps thousands, of persons saw the thing during the five or six minutes it was over the islands. They described it as a circular, glowing object, which seemed to spray a fan of soft white light behind it.

Two Hawaiian National Guard pilots, flying jets that night, also saw it and reported that it was far above their forty-thousand-foot altitude. Lieutenant George Joy said the UFO was leaving a faintly glowing vapor trail. An unidentified spokesman for the Federal Aviation Authority told newsmen that the thing he and his co-workers saw resembled the one described by the pilots.

It was certainly not a satellite and it was in view much too long to have been a meteor or a missile. The evidence from credible and authoritative witnesses indicates that it was another of the strange unidentified aerial craft that constitute one of the most baffling riddles of our time.

22

The Coffins Are Restless Tonight!

The island of Oesel in the Baltic is small, windswept, and rocky. It is best known for the whiskey it exports—and for the unsolved mystery of the Arensburg graves.

Arensburg is the only town on the island. It is customary for the wealthier families to build private chapels where the heavy oak coffins can be kept for a time before they are transferred to the adjoining vault for final burial.

A highway runs alongside the cemetery, and from this road several of the private chapels are visible. One of them, owned by the Buxhoewden family, is nearest the road—and it was in it that the puzzling disturbances were recorded.

Our minister to Naples, Robert Dale Owen, made the matter the subject of a lengthy report, basing it on the testimony of the family of Baron De Guldenstubbe, one of the principals involved.

Summarized from the Owen-Guldenstubbe report, here is the strange story of the restless dead of Arensburg:

On Monday, June 22, 1844, the wife of a tailor named Dalmann drove to the cemetery to visit the grave of her mother. She had her two small children with her in the cart and she hitched the horse to a post in front of the Buxhoewden family chapel. When she returned to the cart a few minutes later she found the horse in a very excited state, heavily lathered and apparently terrorized. Since she could not drive the horse in such a condition, she summoned a veterinarian, who applied the universal remedy of those days—he bled the animal.

Mrs. Dalmann made a trip to tell her strange story to Baron De Guldenstubbe, at his chateau near Arensburg. He was polite—but he was also quite unmoved by this foolish story of an excited horse. He tried to explain to the woman that perhaps the animal had been stung by a bee—or perhaps it had been frightened by a small animal. Old mares are cantankerous, you know.

Their conversation ended with neither impressing the other.

On the following Sunday several persons who had tied their horses alongside the Buxhoewden chapel came from the church services to find the animals quivering with terror. A few days later villagers who passed by that same spot reported that they could hear heavy rumbling sounds coming from the vault below the family chapel. Days passed and more horses became frightened at the same place and in the same manner. Something most unusual was occurring here—of that the officials were agreed—but what was it?

There was so much talk and so much wild exaggeration that something had to be done. Perhaps the answer would be to conduct an official investigation and bring this vexatious matter to an end once and for all.

At first the Buxhoewden family opposed the idea of a probe. They argued that the whole thing was simply the scheme of some enemy of their family who wished to make them look silly. Before they would even consider the idea of an official investigation, they chose several members of their own family to visit the chapel, inspect the vault, and then to let the officials see that there was nothing to investigate but a lot of silly rumors.

The family investigators found a surprise awaiting them. The coffins in the vault were piled in the center of the floor. None had been opened—but all had been moved.

The inspection party patiently lifted the heavy coffins back into place on the iron racks around the walls of the vault. They took extra care to lock the door, even pouring lead into the seals as an extra precaution against tampering.

For several days all was routine there. No more reports of eerie sounds or of terrified horses. Then, on the third Sunday in July, the storm broke.

Eleven horses were tethered in front of the Buxhoewden chapel while their owners attended services. Passers-by found the horses rearing and plunging for no visible reason —in some cases the horses were throwing themselves violently to earth as they sought to break their hitching lines. By the time the alarm was spread, six of the horses were down and could not get up; the others were "saved" by that standard procedure—bleeding. Three of the horses died where they lay—but whether from the fright or the bleeding is not recorded—or admitted.

Those who had lost their horses in this peculiar incident were joined soon by other angry and alarmed citizens in a plea to the Consistory—a church court which sat periodically at Arensburg. The Consistory was as confused as the civil officials; it could not decide what to do, if anything, and while it dawdled, fate stepped in again.

In the midst of this excitement a member of the Buxhoewden family died. After the funeral services, several members of the family decided to visit the vault where such strange doings had been reported. They melted the seals, unlocked the door—and opened it on a scene of utter confusion.

Once again all the coffins were heaped in the center of the floor—some of them upside down. One heavy box was battered as though it had been thrown violently from its resting place on the iron racks. Something—or somebody—had removed those coffins from the customary niches and had tumbled them about before dumping them into the floor in the middle of the vault.

The bewildered members of the family again restored the coffins to the iron racks—again locked the door and poured fresh lead into the seals—and again kept their fingers crossed, wondering what came next.

The word of what had been found got around the island and no doubt became exaggerated in the telling. It soon became clear to the Consistory that they had to take action —some action—whether or no; for this whole business was getting out of hand. Being a committee, the Consistory took the customary committee action: They decided to investigate. The Buxhoewden family still opposed a probe of their family vault, contending that nothing had been found that constituted a menace to the public welfare; but acknowledging that what had been found was something that made the family look foolish if publicized. Hence—they preferred no investigation.

Some cool head in the family reminded them that they were in an excellent position to end this foolishness in their own favor by permitting an investigation at once. Had they not just replaced the coffins themselves and had they not locked and sealed the door themselves? Now, he argued, was the best of all possible times to have the investigation—when all was in order.

The balky Buxhoewdens finally recognized the virtue of his arguments and they startled the Consistory by *asking* for an official investigation—at once.

They got it. But they reckoned without their riddle.

Baron De Guldenstubbe, President of the Consistory, visited the vault with two members of the Buxhoewden family. The door was locked. The seals had not been touched. But when they opened the door, they again found the coffins asunder. The badly shaken party replaced the coffins and resealed the door. Now the die was cast: There had to be a full investigation of this case at once—the local officials must be invited to participate.

Baron De Guldenstubbe asked the church to select a bishop to serve in the probe, and this was done. Also involved were the burgomaster, another town official, a physician—Dr. Luce—and a secretary to take down what was seen and said.

The committee found the locks and seals intact. They also found the coffins heaped in the center of the vault—except that this time the caskets of a grandmother and two small children had not been moved. None of the boxes showed any signs of tampering, but the committee decided to open two of them to ascertain if robbery had been the motive for these strange molestations. Their suspicions were groundless. The jewelry on the bodies they examined had not been removed. They re-sealed the coffins.

How had the intruders entered?

Since the door locks and seals had not been disturbed, the investigators suspected that someone might have tunneled into the vault, bypassing the normal entrance entirely. They brought in workmen, who dug up the floor of the vault and found nothing. Then they dug a deep trench around the entire vault—again without result. Completely baffled by this time, the committee decided that possibly they had been wrong after all—perhaps the intruders *had* entered through the doors.

So they laid an ingenious trap for the ghouls, whoever they might be. They sprinkled fine wood ashes over the floor of the crypt. They locked and sealed the door. They sprinkled more fine wood ashes on the steps leading to the chapel. Then, to make doubly sure that this grisly business was terminated, they posted armed guards beside the vault door for seventy-two consecutive hours.

The guards saw nothing unusual—heard nothing unusual.

The secretary for the committee duly noted the reports and the names of the guards. Then the committee marched down the steps, where the wood ashes were undisturbed. They broke the seals and unlocked the doors.

This time most of the coffins were standing on end, heads down, across the room from where the committee had left them three days before. Once more, only the boxes containing the grandmother and the two children were unmoved.

Again the committee assured itself that there had been no robbery . . . and no secret entrance. Having done all that could be expected of them in this struggle with the mysterious, the committee recommended that the coffins be removed and buried elsewhere—which the Buxhoew-dens were glad to do.

The strange disturbances in the Buxhoewden vault on Oesel Island are paralleled by those reported in the church records at Stanton, in Suffolk County, England.

There, in a vault belonging to the French family, the coffins were placed on heavy wooden biers. But when the vault was opened for an additional interment in 1755, the church record says that there was great astonishment, for the coffins were all disarranged.

One of them, described as a large lead-covered box which required eight strong men to lift, was discovered on the side of the vault opposite the one on which it had originally been placed. It was lying tilted on the fourth step of the stairs leading out of the crypt.

The disturbance had been brought about without breaking the locks or seals on the door.

Additional reading: The investigation by the British government of disturbances centering in the tomb of the Chase family in Barbados, Christ Church graveyard, 1820. And the report on the disturbance in the tomb of Sir Alexander Evan MacGregor, also in Barbados, August, 1943. Both these cases are reported in detail in my book *Stranger Than Science* published by Citadel Press, 1983.

23

Giant in the Sky

Many students of such matters are convinced that the earth has been under systematic and intensive surveillance for a long time. Numerous scientists, both in and out of government, have hinted at this. Let us consider one of the major pieces of evidence:

The steamship *Llandovery Castle* left Mombasa on the last day of June, 1947, bound for Cape Town. On the night of July 1, the ship was passing through the Straits of Madagascar. The time was about 11 P.M., when the lookout and some of the passengers noticed a brilliant light approaching rapidly, overtaking the ship and losing altitude as it did so. The light lost speed and descended to within fifty feet of the water. Then the light turned downward, a brilliant searching beam that cast a diminishing circle on the surface of the sea as the object matched its speed with that of the ship. Suddenly the searchlight beam went out . . . and then the object itself became visible.

All aboard the vessel who saw the thing agreed that it was a gigantic cylindrical craft of some sort, apparently metallic and about five times as long as its diameter. It looked, said the witnesses, like a huge steel cigar with the end clipped. No windows or portholes could be seen; but, from the ease and precision with which it matched its speed to that of the steamship and from the use of the searchlight, it was quite apparent that the craft was under intelligent control of some sort. The size of the craft was nothing less than gigantic; for the witnesses, including some of the ship's officers, estimated that the thing which paced them was three to four times as long as the steamship . . . which meant that it would have been in excess of one thousand feet long and about two hundred feet in diameter.

After cruising along beside the *Llandovery Castle* for perhaps a minute, the gigantic structure began to rise silently until it was about a thousand feet above the water, then great orange streamers of flame shot from the rear of the craft and it leapt forward, rising rapidly to lose itself in the night skies. The incident was duly recorded in the ship's log, and promptly forgotten except by those who saw it.

24

Sam Frame's
Guardian Angel

Perhaps when you are driving near Staunton, Virginia, you might like to make a short side trip to examine this oddity, which is a tombstone about seven miles from that city, on the site of Samuel Frame's old farm.

Frame and his neighbors were accustomed to take their grain, which was generally wheat, to a mill operated by a man named Palmer. They had stored their grain at the mill as usual in 1870, waiting for the fall rains to raise the river so that Palmer could grind their wheat into flour.

But on the night after Frame took his grain to the mill for storage, he had a vivid dream. He told his family next morning that he had dreamed of a "lady in a bright gown" who warned him to remove his grain soon; for a flood would destroy the mill. Frame hurried back to the mill next day and removed his grain. When he urged his friends to heed the warning and remove their grain, too, they hooted at him. That night there was a veritable cloudburst which swept away the mill and everything in it, exactly as the "bright lady" in the dream had predicted.

On Frame's tombstone there is this legend:

"Samuel Frame, buried on this farm. He was warned by an angel in a dream, September 22, 1870, to remove his wheat from Palmer's Mill, now Spring Hill, which he did the following day."

On the island of Jamaica there is a tombstone which says: "Here lies the body of Lewis Galdy, Esquire, who died on the 22nd day of 1737 at the age of 80. He was born in Montpelier in France, which place he left because of his religion and settled on this island, where, in the great earthquake of 1672, he was swallowed up by the earth. But by the wonderful providence of God he was thrown out of the earth and into the sea by a second shock. He continued to swim until he was seen and taken up by a boat and he was thus miraculously preserved."

Of somewhat different tone is the tombstone of one Simantha Lemmer, in the church graveyard at Provincetown, Massachusetts. It reads: "Simantha Lemmer, wife and mother of my nine children. Her heart was good but she made my life a burden with her scolding. On June 4, 1771, she was taken up by the Lord. It is well."

25

Can Dreams
Foretell the Future?

As every researcher into such matters soon learns, the phenomenon of precognitive dreams is the most common type of all inexplicable mental experiences. Because of its very nature, it is the least understood and one of the most difficult to study. The wonderland of the human mind contains many secrets which defy research and which will continue to defy research until better tools are available. Progress is being made, but the work is tedious and the advances microscopic.

It would take many books the size of this one to record each year's crop of dreams which seem to be previews of reality. We can set forth here only a few of the cases which merit special attention because they could be substantiated.

Let us consider the strange case of Mrs. Winnie Wilkinson of Sheffield, England, who lay down to take a nap one afternoon in the summer of 1962. This was unusual for her because she was seldom able to sleep in the daytime. It was unusual in another respect; for she not only slept but she also had a dream, and she seldom dreamed.

In the account which she subsequently gave to police

and other interested officials, Mrs. Wilkinson said that she dreamed of hearing a heavy and persistent pounding on her front door. When she opened the door (in the dream) she was greeted by an excited woman whom she had never seen before. The woman told Mrs. Wilkinson that Mr. Wilkinson had just fallen from a scaffold and was badly injured and that he wanted his wife to come at once.

At that point Mrs. Wilkinson awakened. Although she and her husband had been separated for six months and were contemplating a divorce, she was quite upset by the strange dream. She noted the time, 3:12 P.M. She phoned his employers and was assured that there had been no accident.

On the following day, at 3:12 P.M., Gordon Wilkinson was killed when the scaffold on which he was working suddenly collapsed.

In the spring of 1915 the eminent British lecturer, I. B. S. Holbourne, was returning from a highly successful lecture tour of the United States. He had booked passage on the big Cunard liner *Lusitania,* a fine vessel and a fast one.

Sometime during the early hours of May 7, 1915, the professor's wife, Marion, was sitting in an easy chair in the library of their home. She dozed off and dreamed —a rather disturbing experience under the circumstances; for she seemed to be aboard a huge ocean liner that was in dire straits. The vessel was listing badly. Lifeboats were being launched. People were milling about excitedly but there was no panic and no rioting. Mrs. Holbourne seemed to be standing on the upper deck of the sinking ship and, when a young ship's officer came by, she inquired of him whether her husband was aboard. The officer promptly replied that Professor Holbourne had already left the ship in one of the lifeboats. With that she suddenly found herself back in the library of her home, wide awake and quite alarmed.

At breakfast that morning she discussed the dream with her family and they all laughed at her—"just another nightmare!" they called it.

Hours later their views changed as the news came that the mighty *Lusitania* had been sunk by action of a German submarine off the Irish coast with heavy loss of life. Professor Holbourne, they learned later, had helped many others into life jackets and boats before he was finally ordered from the ship himself. The Professor was a survivor and, from Marion Holbourne's description of the young officer she had questioned in her dream, the Professor was easily able to identify him as the one who had actually ordered him into the lifeboat—just as the officer had told Mrs. Holbourne in her strange dream.

Joseph Ammer's shoe repair shop was located in a run-down section of Indianapolis where price was doubly important. Joe did good work and he was well liked—a quiet, friendly little fellow who was always willing to do a favor. All went well for Joe and his wife, Ruth, and their son Oscar, who graduated with honors from high school, an outstanding athlete of whom his father was very proud.

All went well until the blazing hot afternoon of August 7, 1962. On that day the 67-year-old Syrian did not come home for lunch as usual. His wife awakened from a nap in which she had had a terrible nightmare. She told police later that she had seen her husband struggling with a man who repeatedly wielded a hammer before running from the shop.

Mrs. Ammer awakened and looked at the clock. Her husband was long overdue for his lunch; but perhaps he had stayed at his bench to finish some rush job for a customer, as he often did. She waited another half hour and could not get that alarming dream out of her mind. She put some food into a basket and hurried to the cobbler's shop, only a few blocks away.

The door was standing wide open, not unusual in such hot weather. On the floor behind the counter was the body of Joe Ammer. His hands had been tied behind his back with cobbler's twine, and then he had been brutally beaten to death with a hammer which lay nearby. Missing from the till were a few dollars—for which a man had given his life.

Police reluctantly listened to the distraught woman's description of the killer she had seen in her dream a few hours before. Oddly, they got a tip that a man answering the description given by Mrs. Ammer had been seen washing blood off his hands in a tavern restroom a few minutes after the time of Ammer's slaying. The suspect was not only dressed as Mrs. Ammer had described but he looked like the man in her strange dream.

The trial of William Edmonds took place in May of 1963 in the courthouse at Indianapolis. Of course Mrs. Ammer's dream was not admissible as testimony, although it had played a certain part in the case. The defense attorney contended that the defendant had been too full of drugs to know what he was doing at the time of the slaying, but the jury found Edmonds guilty as charged and he was duly sentenced to spend the rest of his life in prison—for a murder which the widow had watched in her dream.

Similar in its portent to that of Mrs. Ammer was the dream of Mrs. Ernest Topp of East Orange, New Jersey

In May of 1938 Mrs. Topp dreamed that she had seen her husband stabbed to death by a small, long-haired man wielding a butcher knife. Mr. Topp, a veteran cook on the steamship *City of Norfolk,* laughed at his wife's dream. He flatly refused to heed her pleas that he not make the next voyage on the vessel as he was already booked to do. Poppycock! he called the dream.

Mrs. Topp was so disturbed by her nightmare that she told her family and neighbors about it and prevailed upon them to urge her husband not to make the trip. Some of them tried but they got no further than she had. By and large they just scoffed at her and told her that her nightmare was the natural aftermath of an upset stomach—a standard "explanation" which explains nothing.

Ernest Topp sailed on schedule. On the night of May 16, 1938, while the *City of Norfolk* was en route to London, Mrs. Topp had another dream and again she saw her husband stabbed to death in a fight with a short man with long black hair. She woke up screaming, "Don't touch the body until I see it!" Her clock showed that it was 5 A.M.

On the afternoon of that same day she received a cable from the vessel, which had just docked in London. It notified her that her husband had been stabbed to death by a Spaniard named Christ Magurrio. The killer then jumped overboard, and three crewmen who tried to rescue him lost their lives with him when their boat capsized in the stormy seas.

The details of the fatal fight, provided to Mrs. Topp by the shipowners, coincided exactly with those of the fights she had seen in her dreams.

Paolo Grillo was a farmer who had lived all his sixty-three years on a little plot of ground near Treviglano, which is in the Province of Bergamo, Italy.

On the morning of November 27, 1952, Paolo did not go to work in his fields as was his custom. Instead, he went about all morning among his neighbors, telling them of a strange dream he had had the night before.

"Last night," he said, "I dreamed of a very good friend who was with me in the trenches during World War I. I was beside him when he was killed by a sniper's bullet —he died in my arms. In my dream last night he came and stood beside my bed. He touched me on the hand till I looked up and then he said, "Be ready, Grillo. Today you will come with me.""

Grillo's friends tried to assure him that he was worrying about something that had no meaning. Everyone, they said, has bad dreams from time to time. Some of them even recounted the dreams they had experienced which came to naught.

Grillo went away, shaking his head. The day was bright and sunny and warm. His fields needed tending, but Grillo decided it might be bad luck to work that day—he would just spend the afternoon sitting in his old chair leaning back against the front of his cottage.

At sundown that was where they found him—dead of a heart attack.

Sir Henry Wilson will be found listed in the history books as Chief of the British General Staff during the early part of World War I. The later phases of his distinguished career included service as a member of Parliament representing North Down, Ireland. Since he was a long-time friend of Lady Londonderry, a fashionable London socialite, it was only natural that she should go to considerable pains to invite him to a dinner party to be given at her home in June of 1922. Sir Henry was located at a remote hunting lodge in Scotland, thus becoming the last, and thirteenth, guest to be invited. Sir Henry probably would not have been dismayed at being number thirteen, nor did the hostess give it a second thought. Neither of them was superstitious. Perhaps it would have been better if they had been.

At the dinner Sir Henry was in civilian clothes, which were then customary attire for him; and he was in excellent spirits, joking and laughing, which was somewhat unusual in his case. The dinner was a great success and it was almost 2 A.M. before the hostess was able to retire, exhausted but happy.

That night Lady Londonderry, who seldom dreamed, had a vivid and unforgettable dream.

She saw Sir Henry Wilson, in full-dress military uniform, entering a taxi. He was alone in the back seat of the vehicle. She followed it through the streets of London, most of them familiar to her, until the taxi stopped in front of Sir Henry's own residence, which Lady Londonderry instantly recognized. Sir Henry got out, straightened his uniform, paid the driver and then walked briskly to his door as the taxi pulled away down the street. He was leaning forward to insert the key in the door when two men slipped from behind a nearby pillar and ran toward him, pulling pistols from beneath their coats. Lady Londonderry tried to shout a warning but could make no sound. The General heard the footsteps; but, before he could turn, one of the attackers fired at point-blank range. A red blotch appeared on the uniform between Sir Henry's shoulder blades. The General sagged, grabbed a post with his left hand, and pulled his short ceremonial sword from its scabbard with the other hand. As he turned to face his attackers, several more shots rang out and Sir Henry slumped to the steps and lay still. The gunmen fled down the street, and Lady Londonderry woke up, bathed in perspiration, screaming.

Her husband came running to her and the distraught woman told him of her terrifying dream. He tried to calm her by assuring her that it bore no relation to reality, that it was just a dream and nothing more. Finally, to bring the episode to an end, he made a trumped-up call to Sir Henry's residence, and he was assured that the General was sleeping soundly.

But Lady Londonderry could not rid herself of the conviction that somehow she had witnessed a preview of Sir Henry being murdered. She told several friends about it, but all of them advised her to forget it and, above all, not to bother Sir Henry about such a preposterous incident.

Can Dreams Foretell the Future?

Ten days after Lady Londonderry's much-discussed dream, Sir Henry Wilson, as befitted his war record, was selected to unveil the War Memorial at Paddington Station. In keeping with the nature of the event, Sir Henry appeared in full-dress military uniform. After the ceremony was over, he entered a taxi alone and returned to his home.

Sixty seconds after he paid the taxi driver and walked to his own door, Sir Henry Wilson was lying face down on the steps, one hand clutching the handle of his ceremonial sword. He had been shot to death by two gunmen who fled the scene, exactly as Lady Londonderry had seen it in her dream.

Upon rare occasions, dreams of disaster have gratifying endings. Take the case of Julius Dittman, and the dream he had in April of 1956.

Mr. Dittman's store was at Huron Road and Ontario Street, in Cleveland, Ohio, and at that time the Cleveland Parkamatic Corporation had begun construction of a huge parking structure right next door to Mr. Dittman's store.

He had a dream that the parking garage had suddenly collapsed on his store, crushing it into rubble. The dream was so vivid that the next morning Mr. Dittman got in touch with an insurance broker, who gladly sold him a policy which provided up to $120,000 for interruption of business. The policy was delivered to Dittman on Friday, April 6, 1956, at 3 P.M.

On Saturday morning, April 7, at 7 A.M., the new parking building began to sag. Construction engineers were rushed in and they shored up the structure. The top of the tall parking building was hanging out eight feet over the roof of Dittman's store.

The city ordered the new building torn down; ordered Dittman's store closed during the demolition.

The insurance company had to pay off, of course, thanks to the warning Dittman had in his dream.

26

Hardly a
Cloud in the Sky

Mrs. R. Babington of Alexandria, Louisiana, drove into her driveway at about 2:45 P.M. on November 11, 1958, and parked her car. As she started toward the back door of her home she heard the patter of water, striking the lawn and tapping gently on the roof of her home. There was nothing really noteworthy about that, even though the sun was shining and it certainly wasn't raining. She decided it was only some splash-over from a sprinkler in the neighbors' lawn.

Trouble was that her neighbors were not sprinkling, but the water continued to stream down. Pipe burst, perhaps? Examination revealed that all the piping was in good order and no hoses or outside faucets were turned on. Now it was becoming interesting.

Mrs. J. T. Sumrall, who lived across the street, noticed Mrs. Babington circling the house and came out to see what was wrong. She, too, could see the drops of water glistening in the clear still air as they streamed down from nowhere onto the house.

Adras LaBorde, managing editor of the ALEXANDRIA DAILY TOWN TALK, was summoned to the scene by some of the dozens of persons who had gathered to watch this phenomenon. LaBorde observed that the water could not be coming from the leaves of trees because the trees were leafless at that time. By sighting against a twenty-five-foot-high evergreen in the yard, however, he and the others could see that the rain was indeed coming from somewhere high above the house and that it was falling in an area about one hundred feet square—and nowhere else! For two and a half hours the water streamed down and then, as suddenly as it began, the downpour stopped and the crowds went away to wonder.

Neither the nearby England Air Base nor the Weather Bureau could explain how it rained out of a clear sky—nor why it should rain for hours on just one spot of such relatively small size.

Again, it was a type of phenomenon which is rare but not unprecedented.

Dawson, Georgia, was the scene of a downpour from a clear sky in the second week of September, 1866. Not a cloud in the sky, but the water streamed down like a spring rain for more than an hour on a spot not more than twenty-five feet in diameter.

Four times during one week in October, 1886, rain peppered down for hours on just one house and its surrounding lawn, to the great mystification of the folks in Charleston, South Carolina. Since the sky was cloudless during this precipitation, the CHARLESTON NEWS AND COURIER found the inevitable expert who, without visiting the scene of the event, pronounced it nothing more than the dribbling of insects in the trees. Reporters who went to see for themselves found the water peppering down, hour after hour, on the trees, around the trees, and on top of the house. They may be pardoned if they concluded that the dribbling came not from the insects, but from the expert.

In the NEW YORK SUN under date of October 24, 1886, will be found a brief but interesting account of the strange rain which was plaguing a small area in Chesterfield County, South Carolina. For fourteen days the rain fell almost continuously on that one little sector and it came down with such intensity that the drainpipes were kept gushing to carry it from the roofs. Where it came from is not known, for all during that period the skies were cloudless and sunny.

Rain on the roof, even from a clear sky, is baffling but it can be tolerated. However, when it begins to rain *inside* the house—well, that's a different matter!

Dr. and Mrs. William Waterman lived in a nice eight-room house near Windsor, Vermont, when their troubles began in September of 1955.

The first inkling they had of the impending time of trial was the discovery one morning that a strange dew or heavy mist was collecting on just about everything in the house. It stood in bright shiny beads, like perspiration, on the arms of chairs and on the woodwork. The Watermans sought to deal with it by sponging it off—a procedure that left them right where they started, after they carried out thirteen buckets of water in the first two days.

Needless to say, the doctor and his wife were at a loss to understand why such a thing was happening in the house where they had spent nine trouble-free years. The doctor reported that one day, as he transferred a shallow dish of grapes from one room to another, it filled with water during the transit.

As was to be expected, they sought expert help. Electricians could find nothing wrong with any appliances. The insulation and the plumbing checked out, too; in fact, the plaster and insulation were quite dry. The water pipes were not sweating from contact with the air. There were no leaks and no seepage—just that inexplicable collection of water on everything in the house, hour after hour.

The well-watered Watermans moved their clothing and furniture out of the house to dry and moved themselves into a trailer until the plague of indoor rain finally ceased and the house became livable once more.

Ed Mootz saw the cloud that killed his peach trees.

He was mowing the terraced lawn of his home at 440 Boal Street, Cincinnati, Ohio, about 5:30 on the morning of July 22, 1955. It was just a pleasant summer morning and Ed wanted to get that lawn manicured before the sun got too hot for him.

There was nothing unusual about his work until he knelt beside a small peach tree to pull up some weeds that the mower could not reach. As he reached out to grab a handful of weeds, a few reddish drops fell on the back of his hand. The substance was warm and sticky. It looked and felt like watery blood except that it was oily to the touch. A moment later the stuff was pattering down all around him, thicker in texture and even darker red than blood. It was literally raining—like being caught in a warm shower, as he described it later.

Mootz backed away and looked up. There, about a thousand feet overhead, was a small cloud unlike anything he had ever seen before. It was a mixture of red and green and pink and seemed to be rolling. The red in the cloud was the color of the stuff that was raining down on his peach tree. In fact, he could see the drops falling from the direction of the cloud, sort of a smoky leg that broke into droplets as high as he could distinguish them.

At this point Mr. Mootz noticed that the red stuff on his hands was burning him—as a strong antiseptic in an open cut might do. He ran into the house and washed his hands with soap and warm water and had no difficulty getting rid of the strange substance. When he went back outside, the cloud was nowhere in sight and he finished mowing the lawn.

Next morning Mr. Mootz discovered episode two of his bizarre experience: Every one of his six healthy young peach trees had died during the previous twenty-four hours. The leaves were brown and most of them had fallen off. The fruit, about the size of hens' eggs the day before, was shriveled tightly around the seeds. The tree trunks were shriveled and hard, and the grass around and under the peach trees was dead where the mysterious red rain had fallen on it.

There were no planes in the area at the time of the incident and, even had there been, they could not have dropped any liquids into such a restricted pattern. Nor does Mr. Mootz accept the suggestion that some chemical plant might have discharged a cloud of waste matter that somehow hovered over his peach trees for a few minutes.

The bewilderment of Ed Mootz was only equaled by that of the various experts who came and listened and took samples and left. That group included the United States Air Force, which sent representatives to take up the trees and collect the dead peaches and grass, and, above all, to question Mr. Mootz until he had his fill. They took all he could furnish and gave him nothing in return—not even a hint as to why they were so intensely interested in the strange looking cloud that killed his peach trees with a stinging red rain.

27

The Unsinkable Swede

The annals of the sea contain many instances of men being washed overboard during violent storms. There are also numerous well-attested cases where men have been washed off the decks of a ship by one wave—and washed right back on again by the next wave. But for the hapless seaman who goes overboard in fog—at night—without being missed immediately, the chances of rescue are less than astronomical—they are virtually nil.

Let us examine the incredible case of a young Swedish sailor named Per Svahlin and the strange fate which befell him on the night of October 28, 1962. Svahlin was assigned to lookout on the bow of the 577-foot freighter *Horn Crusader*. It was an important post, for the *Crusader* was creeping through the fog about twenty miles off Santa Barbara, California, and the danger of collision was very real.

Five minutes before 9 P.M. it was discovered that Svahlin was missing. A search of the vessel was begun at once. By 9:30 Captain Alfred Johansen was convinced that the young Swede had fallen overboard in the dense fog and darkness.

Without hesitation Captain Johansen slowly swung the big freighter around and *endeavored* to retrace his path to the point where Svahlin had last been seen on duty. Unable to steer by the stars, he managed to navigate by using his radar to bounce signals off the shore—and by compass.

How long had Svahlin been in the water? Nobody knew, but he had been missing for at least forty minutes when the ship turned around to start the search. Captain Johansen knew that he had little chance of finding the man, even if he still lived, but he was determined to try.

Mile by mile the *Horn Crusader* picked her way through the fog. They blew the whistle. They listened. They heard nothing. At 10:05 Captain Johansen felt a strong urge to alter the course of the vessel seven degrees to starboard. Minutes later the lookout heard Svahlin yelling. He was only thirty yards from the ship, weak, but very much alive. Somehow, Captain Johansen had navigated his ship more than nine miles through fog and darkness and *had* found a lone swimmer in the sea!

28

Miracle Cures

James Lenehan of Philadelphia was nineteen years old in 1949, and like most youngsters he felt that he could take chances beyond reason—and get away with it. Perhaps he felt that nothing serious could happen to him because it never had. James was wrong.

He was riding on the running board of an automobile —a dangerous procedure—and he was thrown from it against a telephone pole. A police ambulance rushed him to Bryn Mawr Hospital, where he lay unconscious for nine days. Even after he regained consciousness, the doctors told his parents that James could not possibly live because of the extent and nature of his injuries. Believing that the lad was dying, his mother placed in the boy's hand a shred of cloth from the church robes of the late Bishop John Neumann, who died many years ago in Philadelphia.

Five weeks later James Lenehan, the lad who could not recover, was discharged from Bryn Mawr Hospital—his only defect a deafness in the left ear. The late Bishop Neumann has been approved for beatification, in part because of the miraculous recovery of James Lenehan.

In 1957, Linda Crockett of Liverpool was stricken with

hepatitis. In spite of everything that could be done for her by medical science, the child's condition worsened. Finally the doctors told the parents that Linda could not live through the night. About midnight the father dropped off to sleep in his chair beside the bed of the dying child, but Linda's mother knelt and began to pray. Shortly after 1 A.M. the little girl called her mother and the mother bent over the child. Linda said: "Mother, you can stop praying now. I'm going to be all right—that lady in the bright nightgown who has been standing there beside you just told me."

The doctors were wrong . . . and Linda was right; for within a week she was fully recovered and by 1963, at the age of fifteen, she had become a normal, healthy young lady, whose parents attribute her survival to the power of prayer.

29

Howard Wheeler's Enigma

Howard Wheeler, a broadcaster in Charlotte, North Carolina, is a very devout man. Sunday, June 10, 1962, is a day he will long remember, for it brought him an experience that defies explanation.

He had had a good day and was ready for bed. It was about one o'clock on Sunday morning and Howard was kneeling beside the bed saying his prayers. Suddenly he stopped and said to his wife, "Pat, I heard an automobile wreck! I'll be right back!"

Howard later said that it had not sounded like the conventional grinding crash of a car wreck, but more like the distant rumble of railroad cars bumping together in some freight yard.

When Howard Wheeler got out of the house and into his car, there was a major decision to be made and nothing on which to base his judgment: Where was the wreck—if there was one? There were many streets around his home, and almost any of them would have been a good prospect for an automobile crackup. Which one should he take? Without hesitation Howard sped down Park Road. When he came to Woodlawn, he drove right on down the hill to the shrimp boat. Nothing there. Then, for some reason he could not explain, he got the feeling that he should turn around and hurry back to Montford Drive . . . which he did.

In recounting Wheeler's bizarre experiences the CHARLOTTE NEWS says: "He went about 200 yards on Montford, around a curve and there was a car smashed against a pole—the engine driven back into the car. He saw no one . . . but a voice said: 'Help me, Humpy, help me!' "

Pinned in the wreck, badly hurt and bleeding, was Joe Funderburke, an old acquaintance who always called Wheeler by the nickname of Humpy. Wheeler managed to get him out of the wreckage and to the hospital, where emergency surgery was performed. *How* did Wheeler hear that crash, half a mile from his home? *How* did he find it? Not only did he find it and rescue his friend, but forty-five minutes later when the police arrived—Howard Wheeler was still the only passer-by who *had* found the wreck.

30

Strange Hunches

On Christmas Eve of 1958, at about ten in the morning, Mrs. Hazel Lambert of Pennsbury Heights, near Philadelphia, was driving home from her job at the Cartex Corporation. She proceeded as usual along Route 13 and stopped at Delmoor Avenue in Morrisville to let out a fellow worker. Mrs. Lambert then decided to drive to a food market about a block from where her passenger got out.

All of a sudden, as she drove that extra block, Mrs. Lambert had a strange and powerful feeling that something was wrong. For some reason which she could never explain, she turned her car into Franklin street—which does not go past the food market. In fact, she had never before been on Franklin Street.

As she later told the story to newsmen, she felt compelled to continue driving, faster and faster, until she came to the intersection with Hillside Street, which runs along the canal. Looking beyond the intersection to the canal, Mrs. Lambert was horrified to see a pair of children's bright red mittens clutching frantically at the edge of a hole in the ice.

She drove straight through the intersection and over

the curb and right down to the water's edge. She had almost reached the child, when the car broke through the ice and settled in four feet of water—the ice jamming the car doors so that she could not open them. She began screaming and blowing the automobile horn.

George Taylor and his fourteen-year-old son heard the screams and came running, bringing with them a long pole. The boy used the pole to scoot out on the ice so that he could rescue two-year-old Carol Scheese—who owed her life to Mrs. Lambert's strange hunch.

Forty-year-old Charles Bogardus was a veteran police officer of Los Angeles. On a March night of 1959, he was sitting in his home at 3843 South Cimarron Street, examining some insurance papers with his wife.

He shoved the papers aside and looked up at her.

"Mildred," he said, "something is going to happen. But if it happens to me, don't worry. You will be taken care of."

Mrs. Bogardus was taken aback by this fatalistic statement, which was so unlike her husband. Naturally she wanted to know why he talked in that fashion.

"I really don't know. I just have a feeling and it won't go 'way."

A few days later, at three o'clock on the afternoon of April 4, Bogardus and his partner, Officer Norman Comeau, set out on a routine trip in their patrol car. There was nothing of note until 10:40 P.M. Then their car got a radio call to rush to the supermarket at 1451 West Washington Boulevard, where passers-by had seen two gunmen beating up the employees, who were unable to open the time-lock safe.

The officers broke down the door and rushed into the store. Bogardus chased a bandit, Howard Grant, up a flight of stairs. A moment later Bogardus came tumbling back down the stairs with a bullet in the brain.

His grim premonition had come true.

Mrs. Paul Stratas, of Hughson, California, was at work in Modesto in late 1957. All at once she felt an overwhelming compulsion to telephone her home; for she had a hunch that something was amiss there. Unable to resist the impulse any longer she went to the phone. She reached her father, Harry Schulze, and asked him to check on her thirteen-year-old son Nicky. The grandfather hurried over to his daughter's home—but he arrived five minutes too late. Nicky had been riding his bicycle with a loaded shotgun across the handle bars. The gun had fallen, struck the curbing, and discharged, killing Nicky instantly.

Not all hunches come too late to be helpful.

In 1947, Abraham Isser of New York City was the dinner guest of Mr. and Mrs. Clifford Mack at their home, 56 West 54th Street, in New York. At that time Mr. Mack was a magazine publisher and after dinner he and Isser sat down in the living room for a business chat. His wife served some wine and excused herself, explaining that she wished to take a bath.

After the men had been talking about twenty minutes,

Isser had a terrible feeling that something was amiss with Mrs. Mack. He leapt to his feet and shouted, "Break down the bathroom door! Break it down immediately!"

Naturally Mack was startled. Had his guest gone beserk?

Isser again yelled for Mack to break down the bathroom door at once . . ."If you don't," he shouted, "I'll call the police!"

Thoroughly alarmed by this time at Isser's actions, Mack got to his feet and took his guest to the bathroom to show him there was nothing to get excited about. Mack called to his wife. There was no reply. The bathroom door was locked. He called again. Still no reply.

Now it was Mack's turn to get excited. Behind him Isser was yelling to break the door down—for he still had that overpowering feeling of impending disaster.

Mack kicked out the bottom panel of the door, unlocked it, and rushed in—to find that his wife had fainted and her head was under water in the tub. He carried her into the bedroom and applied resuscitation methods until she finally revived.

She fully recovered from the near-tragedy and was alive and well as late as 1952—thanks to Abraham Isser's hunch that she needed help.

31

Baffling Blackouts

The days of mystery are apparently
without end. On February 14, 1963, there was a sudden
and widespread power failure in the city of Denver,
Colorado. It affected more people than any similar failure
in the history of the Public Service Company of that city.
It all began shortly after 11 o'clock in the morning, when
electrical power suddenly ceased to flow between two of
the main stations serving the city of Denver. The blockage
caused an overload of current, which promptly knocked
out relay lines to Cheyenne and Boulder. The Cherokee
plant was quickly shut down to prevent possible damage
to the turbines.

One hour and twenty-two minutes after it began, the
power failure ended itself just as suddenly and just as
mysteriously as it started. High-voltage current began
flowing through the lines again and engineers hastily got
out to patrol the lines and look for the cause. Between
the Zuni and Cherokee plants, close inspection showed
no break of any kind. Other crews double checked all the
equipment and plants in the Denver area. They could
find nothing amiss.

The baffled experts announced that they would continue

their probing until the cause was found, so that steps could be taken to guarantee against recurrence. But a state official later told newsmen: "There is no guarantee that it won't happen again. We may never know what happened and we don't know now!"

You have doubtless noticed that there is little, if anything, that is really new in this strange world of ours. That holds true for blackouts such as the one we have just discussed—there have been others, similar to, if not identical with, the Denver case.

Elsewhere in this book I report on the power failure at the Eureka, Utah, station on the night of April 18, 1962, when the near approach or landing of some large unidentified object coincided with the plant's inability to function.

Coral Lorenzen, director of the Aerial Phenomena Research Organization, reports on still another case in her book, *The Great Flying Saucer Hoax* (APRO, 4145 East Desert Place, Tucson, Arizona, 1962). The case, which she discusses in considerable detail, was researched for her by Dr. Olavo Fontes of Brazil and deals with the night of August 17, 1959, when the four automatic keys in the big electric power station at Uberlandia, Minais Gerais, suddenly turned themselves off. This automatically cut off the flow of power to all trunk lines. Startled technicians checked and found nothing wrong—except that the current could not flow because the keys had broken the circuit.

Before the Chief Engineer could contact the distant substations, one of them called him. The man said that all the keys at the substation had kicked themselves open when a flying saucer passed over the power station at low altitude. The Chief Engineer warned the man about drinking on the job, and hung up.

The Chief then turned on two of the main keys and nothing happened; but when he closed the third key all of them popped open again.

Just then, says Dr. Fontes, there were shouts outside the Uberlandia station—a brilliantly glowing flying saucer was passing overhead, following a path that kept it over the power lines leading in from the substation which was out of business.

As soon as the UFO had passed on out of sight the Uberlandia station could be restored to service and there was no damage to any part of the system.

When the UFO was there—the electricity wasn't.

A power failure that was more prolonged—and more mundane—was that which plagued the electric company at Grass Valley, California, for several weeks in the winter of 1962.

Each evening at about the same time the lights would blink, grow dim, flicker for a few seconds, and then brighten again.

The experts found nothing. But the mystery was finally solved by a farmer who noticed that each evening, about sundown, his big Black Angus bull was scratching its back on a guy wire that led down from a utility pole. The animal's weight caused the power line to short out for a few seconds while the bull leaned on the wire.

32

TV Scans a Monster

While some nations, including our own, are engaged in a frantic and ruinously expensive program to reach the moon, the fact remains that most of the earth has never been seen by man. This is true because oceans cover seventy per cent of the earth; and only five per cent of the ocean bottom has yet been seen by human beings.

The record—a growing record at that—shows that we have much to learn about the ocean and its creatures. One fascinating bit of information was kept under wraps for nine months before it finally came to light . . . the story of the weird creature that frequented the depths off Santa Barbara, California, in February, 1962.

Forrest Adrian, a photographer, was using a television camera directed by remote control to check the point where an underwater oil well casing entered the ocean floor. He was so startled that he yelled when a strange creature like a giant snake appeared on the screen of the set. The whole crew rushed into the cabin and watched it along with Adrian. The deep-sea divers who worked around that wellhead were especially interested, of course.

What they saw was a creature between ten and fifteen

feet long, designed along the general lines of a snake. It had knobby ridges running around the spiral of its body, like a long, coiled spring with lumps on it; and it swam by rolling round and round. As it vanished from camera range and reappeared from time to time, the viewers had the feeling that there were several of the creatures, slightly different in length and bulk . . . although they saw no more than one at a time. It was evidently attracted by the camera lights at a depth of 179 feet.

Scientists, none of whom bothered to go see the thing, ventured the various opinions that it was a member of the jellyfish family, or a group of little creatures that held onto each other, or just a lot of jellyfish clinging to each other, etc. etc. Since this did not satisfy those who HAD seen the critter, the crew of that Shell Oil rig just called the monster Marvin . . . which means . . . "friend of the sea."

That's what the divers hope he is.

33

Mysterious Memorial

The people of Marion, Ohio, have long since become accustomed to the phenomenon of the strange monument which stands in the eastern corner of a cemetery there.

It is an impressive creation, a gracefully tapered white granite column topped with a black granite sphere about three feet in diameter. The memorial was erected in 1897 over the grave of Charles Merchant and six members of his family.

Until July of 1905 it was just another tombstone in a cemetery along with hundreds of others.

On that midsummer morning a workman noticed that the heavy black marble sphere atop the Merchant memorial had been moved. The orb, weighing several hundred pounds, had obviously turned several inches, exposing the rough spot on the bottom of the ball where it had fitted into the top of the column. This could not be the work of pranksters, because the ball is so heavy hat it would take block and tackle gear to lift it.

In an effort to forestall any additional rotation, the cemetery officials poured a lead cement into the recess atop the column, in which the sphere rested. Two months later the big black ball had moved ten inches and once again the base spot was appearing on the lower underside of the sphere, just as it had done before.

Among the swarms of curious who came to watch and wonder were some scientists. One of them, a geologist, considered the evidence and concluded that the movement of the heavy marble ball was the result of unequal expansion, due to one side facing the sunshine while the other side remained relatively cool. Other scientists took issue with this suggestion; for they pointed out that, if expansion due to heat was the cause of the turning, the ball would turn *toward* the south—whereas this one turns in the opposite direction.

After a flurry of articles in newspapers and magazines the mysterious memorial lapsed into limbo. There are still a few who come to examine it and still a few who seek to explain it.

But the black marble ball in the Marion cemetery—like Old Man River—just keeps rolling along.

34

The Navy
Sees a Ghost

On the log book of the old Navy destroyer *Kennison* is the official record of two strange encounters that defy explanation. One occurred during the early winter of 1942 when the *Kennison* was patrolling off the Golden Gate, on the lookout for Japanese submarines. Visibility was poor because of the dense fog that had formed suddenly; and the *Kennison*, inward bound at the time, was groping her way carefully, trusting to her rather primitive radar to spot the Farallon Islands in time to avoid trouble.

Lookout on the galley deck was Howard Brisbane, and the lookout on the after gun deck was a fellow named Tripod. Suddenly the lookout on the fantail, Torpedoman First Class Jack Cornelius, broke in on the intercom and yelled for the other crewmen to look aft—quickly. Then Cornelius called excitedly to alert the bridge. Both Cornelius and Tripod reported that the *Kennison* had been narrowly missed by what appeared to be a derelict two-masted sailing vessel which had plowed across within a few yards of the destroyer's stern. Their descriptions of the thing coincided: a shabby, unmanned sailing vessel of a type long vanished in those waters. It had been in sight for about twenty seconds and both men had seen it —but the radar man had seen no indication of it.

In April of 1943, when the *Kennison* was on guard off San Diego, she was returning to port after convoying the troopship *Lurline* through some sub-infested waters. It was night as the *Kennison* reached a point about 150 miles from San Diego. The sea was glassy smooth and the night was bright with stars. Sailors Carlton Herschell and Howard Brisbane were on lookout watch on the flying bridge. Through binoculars they picked up a freighter plowing toward them and coming fast. They alerted the radar shack . . . but the radar man saw nothing on his scope. By this time the freighter was an estimated seven miles away and visible to both lookouts by the naked eye. Suddenly it was gone . . . another of the phantoms that pass in the night.

35

The Plague of Mold

Fifteen miles northeast of Winston-Salem, North Carolina, is the town of Elkin, and a few miles from there on a narrow gravel road is the farm of Mr. and Mrs. Grady Norman, who were projected into the news in the summer of 1961 as the result of a peculiar pestilence which infested their home.

The Normans purchased a piece of linoleum floor covering from a neighbor who was selling out and leaving the area. They washed the linoleum and tacked it down on two rooms of their home.

Shortly after their new floor covering had been laid, Mrs. Norman noticed that she was suffering from a choking sensation and what seemed to be hay fever. The doctor advised her to give up feather pillows, which she did without any improvement in her condition. Then Mr. Norman began to suffer—and they noticed that their troubles were most acute in the rooms where their new linoleum was on the floor. When they looked under the floor covering, they found a thick layer of gray-green mold. Mr. Norman promptly pulled up the linoleum and took it to the barn. They scrubbed the floors in the affected rooms with detergents and hot water and then shellacked them in the hope that the shellac might control any mold that had escaped the other cleaners.

Their hopes were vain.

Two days later the grayish mold was showing up on the woodwork and on their clothing. A rug became a mass of mold that rose in a choking dust when they walked on it. The walls changed color as the mold spread over them almost overnight. When it got on their skins, it produced a powerful itching and burning sensation.

The beleaguered couple fought back bravely with an array of ammoniated cleaners, with detergents of all sorts, and with sprays galore. It was all futile—the ubiquitous mold seemed to thrive on their efforts. It defied sunlight and fresh air. It spread over pictures on the wall and it infiltrated the pages of the family Bible. Sofas and a couch were ruined in a matter of hours after it first showed up on their coverings. The harrassed Normans were forced to move their belongings piece by piece onto the porch and finally into the yard. And those who had to handle the mold-infested furniture were subjected to racking fits of coughing that lasted for hours.

Finally the story of their plight spread far and wide and the Surry County health authorities forbade anyone to enter the house. They found that the mold could be destroyed by subjecting the affected articles to a bath in solutions of carbolic acid. But that was certainly no cure for the pestilence, for such treatment would ruin many articles as completely as would the mold.

In a last desperate gesture, the Normans moved into an old bus, trying to live in it as best they could with the items given to them by friends, while the health authorities tried to figure out what to do about a house and its contents which had been made uninhabitable, and perhaps dangerous to human life, by a creeping gray mold that had spread over the entire interior of the place in a matter of days, in defiance of man and his vaunted mastery of all he surveys.

At the Norman farm in Surry County, North Carolina, mold was king.

36

Mystery at Midnight

The steamship *Fort Salisbury* was plowing along at a modest seven knots through the Gulf of Guinea off the west coast of Africa on the night of October 28, 1902. It had been an uneventful trip, with a solid ship and a good crew and a profitable cargo in the hold. The equator was only a few hours ahead when the Captain turned out his light and went to bed.

The night was clear and the stars were bright. There was nothing of note until five minutes past three, when the lookout spotted something dead ahead of them in the water, where nothing should have been. He strained his eyes to make certain they were not playing tricks on him; for ship's officers do not like to be called from their bunks in the wee hours to be told that it was all a mistake. But this was no mistake. The lookout shouted the alarm and the pilot took emergency action to miss the thing, if possible.

The second officer, Mr. A. H. Raymer, hurried on deck. He ordered the searchlight switched on, and the long finger of blue light stabbed into the darkness. It quickly picked up a tremendous object of some sort, low in the water, with two small orange-red lights near one end . . . two blue-green lights near the other.

As the *Fort Salisbury* came up to the vast bulk, Officer Raymer sent word to the Captain to come on deck quickly. The *Fort Salisbury* was passing some sort of huge rounded metallic thing, about a hundred feet in diameter and six hundred feet long. From within the object came clanking sounds that indicated the presence of machinery . . . and other noises that sounded like excited voices, but unintelligible to either Raymer or the other crew members who were at the rail with him. It looked, they said, like a great airship made out of metal plates . . . and it was slowly but surely sinking . . . by design or otherwise. Raymer had the ship's lights played on the thing . . and shouted inquiries whether they needed help. There was no sign of recognition . . . just the vast shiny metallic bulk with the tiny lights . . . which gradually slid beneath the waves . . . another riddle of the open seas.

37

Sea Serpent Mysteries Solved?

A denizen of the deep that washed ashore at Venice, California, in December of 1955, bore a marked resemblance to some of the descriptions of weird creatures reported by various ships' crews. The Venice carcass was sixteen feet long, about fourteen inches in diameter, with a snakelike head and fins. It weighed about 800 pounds.

As soon as Joe Korhummel of Redwood City heard of the monster on the beach at Venice he was reminded of the thing that he had seen floundering in the shallows near Redwood, in July of 1955. He saw something struggling in the rocks just off shore and climbed as near as possible to get a better look. What he found did nothing to stabilize his emotions.

Joe suddenly discovered himself looking down on a huge, snakelike creature sixteen to eighteen feet long, brownish-green in color, with a fanlike fin just behind its snaky head. It was at least a foot in diameter and was fighting to free itself from the rocks into which it was wedged. Joe's wife was screaming for him to get away from the wildly threshing monster. Suddenly it occurred to him that she was giving good advice, and he hastened to heed it.

There is a strong resemblance between these two objects and many of the sea serpent reports. There is also a strong resemblance between them and the creature known as the oarfish, which lives at depths of thousands of feet and seldom comes to the surface unless in distress. The oarfish is a long, sinuous creature that sometimes reaches a foot in diameter. It has a ribbon-like fin down its entire length. On top of its snaky looking head two spikes project, like some sort of antenna, which they may be.

There is a mounted specimen of oarfish in the display at the San Diego Museum. It is 22 feet long and it weighed more than 600 pounds when it washed ashore some years ago, one of the few large specimens of the kind ever captured intact. It is quite possible that the snaky looking oarfish may grow to tremendous size; and if it does, it may explain many of the sightings of sea monsters which would otherwise be unexplainable.

PART TWO

Science has found that nothing can disappear without a trace. Nature does not know extinction. All nature knows is transformation.

If God applies this fundamental rule to the most significant and minute parts of His universe, surely it makes sense to assume that He applies it also to the masterpiece of His creations, the human soul. Everything that science has taught me—and continues to teach me—strengthens my belief that there is a spiritual existence after death.

—Wernher Von Braun, 1960

38

Dead Man's Shorthand

One of the strongest bits of evidence for human survival after death is the case of a four-year-old child and the incredible message he wrote. It is a case that was carefully checked and verified by Dr. J. B. Rhine, the noted parapsychology researcher at Duke University.

A young mother suddenly found herself a widow, with a four-year-old son to support and a hotel to operate. The child spent considerable time in the hotel lobby, and one evening, about two weeks after his father's untimely death, the mother noticed that the youngster was scribbling on a pad of paper. After filling three sheets with his scrawls, he placed them in his mother's mailbox.

Next morning one of the desk clerks called the mother's attention to the unusual nature of the child's doodling. The writing looked like shorthand to the clerk; but since neither the mother nor the clerk could read shorthand they showed the papers to the public stenographer in the hotel, who assured them it did indeed resemble shorthand, but a method that is now considered obsolete.

The stenographer, however, was able to translate the characters and as she wrote them down, bit by bit, she discovered that they constituted an intelligible message.

It began with a term of endearment which the child's father had always used in referring to his wife. The message then added that some important papers, including bonds and insurance policies, were in a safe deposit box in a New York bank.

This proved to be correct. The papers were there and their discovery solved a financial crisis which had been precipitated by the father's sudden death.

Perhaps the most astounding facet of this very strange story was the fact that the father had once been a stenographer and had used the obsolete form of shorthand in which the child wrote the message.

If it was a message from beyond the grave it materially strengthens the belief that the human consciousness does survive the death of the body. If it was not a message from beyond the grave then its existence presents still another perplexing question . . what was it?

39

*Had the Boy
Lived Before?*

Pramodh Sharma was born in Bisauli,
District Budaun, India, on March 14, 1944, the second
son of Professor Bankey Lal Sharma, a teacher at Inter-
mediate College.

The boy served notice that he was strangely different
when, at the age of three, he informed his startled parents
that he had decided to drop the name they had given
him and would henceforth be known by his "real" name
which, he said, was Parmanand.

This was only the opening gesture in his remarkable
story. The child began talking at length of Moradabad,
which he had certainly not seen. Of course his parents
had heard reports of children who seemed to have lived
before, including the well-documented and much investigated story of Shanti Devi, who still lives and works in
New Delhi (1963) after learning that her efforts to pick
up a previous existence in Muttra only brought confusion
and heartache to all persons involved. Hearing of such
cases is one thing; finding such a case in one's own family
is quite another and infinitely more difficult.

The Sharma child talked incessantly of Moradabad and

143

compared it with his life as the son of Professor Sharma. He urged the Professor to take him to his "former" home and promised that he would show the Professor the fine bake shop he used to own there and where such good things were to be had, far better than the similar products in Bisauli. The worried parents resisted such proposals as a matter of course, for tradition has it in India that "reincarnated" persons who know of their past existences do not live long.

The turning point came when Parmanand returned home late one day and, to his father's inquiry, he replied that he had just come from Saharanpur. And he added: "My tummy got wet and I died. Now I have come to Bisauli."

Later the boy claimed that he once owned a shop in Moradabad and that he had had four sons and a daughter. He himself had been named Mohan, he said, and had been one of four brothers. His big fat wife, he asserted, still lived at Moradabad—and he urged Professor Sharma to take him to that city where he would show them that what he said was all true.

On August 15, 1949, Professor Sharma, with his son Pramodh (who called himself Parmanand) and some relatives, went to Moradabad by train. The Professor had decided that it was high time to test the child, and to determine whether he could identify any of the places and persons with which he claimed to be familiar.

The boy passed the test with flying colors. Although he had never been to Moradabad (since his birth in Bisauli) he led his father's party unhesitatingly to the shop operated by the Mohan brothers. He took them to the soda water factory which the late Parmanand operated and explained in detail how the carbonating machine worked and how it was made. Rather heady matter for a five-year-old boy!

Since the boy named Pramodh Sharma of Bisauli claimed to have been a man named Parmanand who had lived and died and raised a family in Moradabad, it was natural that he should be called upon to identify, if possible, the members of his alleged family.

Pramodh correctly recognized and named the wife, daughter, and sons of the late Parmanand. He spoke to them of intimate things that no outsider could have known and answered their questions promptly and correctly. Among other things, as he went through the house where Parmanand had lived and died, he pointed out the changes that had been made since Parmanand's death, including two rooms that had been added.

When it came time for him to leave for Bisauli with his father and the other members of the party, the child clung to the members of the family which he claimed to have known before. He had to be forcefully taken from them and left the entire family in tears—confused—but convinced that the parent who had died had somehow returned in the person of this remarkable child.

Pramodh Sharma is alive and well today (1963). He lives with his parents in Bisauli and tries to forget the strange circumstances which seem to tie him to another existence as another individual in another town.

Perhaps you recall that the child, Pramodh, told his puzzled parents: "When I was Parmanand, my tummy got wet and I died."

Investigation disclosed that Parmanand was hospitalized with an undiagnosed abdominal ailment and was given a hot bath shortly before he died.

Parmanand Mohan died at the age of 39 in Moradabad, on May 9, 1943.

Pramodh Sharma was born on March 15, 1944, in Bisauli.

On August 15, 1949, in the presence of many credible witnesses, the child Pramodh gave extensive and indisputable evidence that he had acquired the memories of the late Parmanand—that somehow their lives had become intertwined through the mysteries of death and birth, adding thus another mystery that defies explanation.

The results are plain and unmistakable—only the process eludes us.

40

They Never Came Back

Sometimes when people disappear it seems that they literally walk off the earth. Such was the case with David Lang, whose classic disappearance as he walked across a field in Tennessee was watched by five witnesses. And in my book—*Stranger Than Science*, I also recounted the story of the Eskimo village of Anjikuni, where every man, woman, and child vanished, leaving their guns standing beside the doors of their huts . . . their kayaks to rot on the beaches . . . and their dogs to starve. They vanished without a hint as to how, or where or why they went.

To the list of mysterious disappearances let us add another remarkable case.

July 24, 1924, was just another day of blazing heat in the deserts of the Middle East, then called Mesopotamia. The Arabs were up in arms again; the British were keeping an eye on them whenever possible. On that day Flight Lieutenant W. T. Day and Pilot Officer D. R. Stewart took off in their single engine plane for a routine reconnaisance over the desert. Estimated flying time: four hours.

They have not been seen since.

When their plane was found, the day after they failed to

return, the mystery was only deepened. There was gasoline in the tank, and the engine started readily when tried. There were no signs that the plane had been shot at. There was no clue to hint why they might have landed where they did . . . in a broad stretch of inhospitable desert.

The search party found something else that adds question marks to the case of the missing fliers.

Beside the plane in the soft sand were the boot marks where officers Day and Stewart had jumped down from the craft. Their tracks showed that they had left the plane and walked along side by side for about forty yards. There the tracks ended. The arrangement of the footprints indicated that the men had simply stopped, standing side by side. Then, and there, they vanished.

The fate which befell them will probably never be known. Armored trucks, planes, and half a dozen patrols of native tribesmen scoured the desert for miles around. There was never a trace of the missing fliers. Where their footsteps ended in the sand, their life stories ended too. And there began another classic mystery of missing men, another true story that is, indeed, strangest of all.

41

Impossible Fossils

A party of four prospectors was working the barren hills at the head of Spring Valley near Eureka, Nevada, in July of 1877. They were picking their way through the area step by step, looking for a telltale outcropping of precious metal.

One of the men noticed a peculiar object projecting from a high ledge of rock near the spot where he was breaking samples. Out of curiosity he climbed to a point where he could get a better look at the protrusion and was amazed to find that it looked like the leg bone of a human being, broken off just above the knee. Since it was firmly embedded in solid rock, he got his companions to help him dislodge the portion that held the oddity.

With the aid of some small picks they removed the upper portion of the encasement. The rock was hard as flint and the bones solidly set in it. The quartzite was dark red and the bones were almost black. When the last of the stone had been picked loose, the leg bone and the foot which was still attached stood out perfectly. It had—in addition to about four inches of leg bone above the knee—the knee joint and knee cap, the lower leg bones, and the complete bones of the foot. The men quickly noticed the unusual size of the

149

leg. From knee to heel it was thirty-nine inches; the man who had owned it had been nothing less than a giant.

The miners realized they had a most unusual find. They brought it to Eureka, where it was placed on display in a store window. Doctors who examined the specimen agreed that it was unquestionably human, incredibly old, and certainly the leg of a giant. The Eureka paper wrote several stories about it, some of which were picked up in other parts of the country. Two museums sent representatives to search for the rest of this remarkable skeleton but they went away empty handed. There was just that tantalizing leg bone and foot—nothing more.

Such frustrations are common in the world of the archeologist. In the strip coal mine operated by Captain Lacy near Hammondsville, Ohio, in the autumn of 1868, a workman named James Parsons loosened a huge mass of coal which fell into the pit, revealing a large, smooth, slate wall which was literally covered with hieroglyphics, in lines about three inches apart. Crowds flocked to see this marvel. Local scholars could not read the hieroglyphics. By the time qualified scientists got there with proper equipment, the slate had crumbled in the air and the writing was destroyed.

42

The Incredible Case of
Josiah Wilbarger

The State of Texas has erected a monument which commemorates the deed of a courageous woman—and the dreams which inspired the deed.

Josiah Wilbarger was a school teacher who lived at La Grange, Texas, in 1838. At the time of his incredible experience in that same year he was visiting with his friend, Reuben Hornsby, who lived on a farm near what is now the city of Austin.

Wilbarger liked the idea of settling near Hornsby but first he wanted to look the land over and select a good spot for farming. He rode out one morning with four companions and before they had gone more than a couple of miles one of the group spotted a lone Indian watching them from his horse on a nearby ridge. When the Indian did not return their friendly greetings they decided to investigate, and he fled from the scene with the four of them in pursuit. In a matter of minutes they lost him in the dwarf cedar trees that covered the hillsides.

The men returned to a small creek. There they picketed their horses and, after drinking their fill, sprawled on the ground to rest, a foolish action under the circumstances.

Moments later they were overwhelmed by Indians who burst upon them from the surrounding thicket.

Two of Wilbarger's companions died instantly, before they could get to their feet. Two other white men scrambled to their feet, fired a couple of shots at the howling attackers and dived into the bushes. Wilbarger had already been struck in the back by two arrows, but he managed to join his companions in their headlong flight. There was a rifle shot that sent Wilbarger staggering, blood gushing from his throat. He fell at the feet of his companions, apparently dead, and they left him there as they made good their escape.

The Indians looted and mutilated the bodies of the first two men who had been killed and, when they came to Wilbarger, they stripped him of his clothing and scalped him. Despite the wounds and the brutality, the flame of life still flickered feebly within him.

He evidently lay there unconscious for several hours, for it was nearly dark when he regained his senses. He was covered with blood and was so weak that he could not stand. Naked as he was, the wind rattled his teeth each time that he crawled from the shelter of the brush. Yet Wilbarger was determined to live—determined to reach the home of the Hornsby's, about six miles from where he lay. He dragged himself painfully along for about a quarter of a mile and then he collapsed.

As he lay there, only half-conscious, bloody and battered, he had a strange experience. It seemed to be a dream. His sister, who lived in Missouri, stood before him and said: "Brother Josiah, you are too weak to go on by yourself.

Remain here where you are and friends will come to take care of you before the setting of the sun."

Wilbarger pleaded with his sister to remain with him. Instead, she shook her head and smiled sadly as she moved away in the direction of the Hornsby's home.

Wilbarger's companions had made their way to Hornsby's, where they had reported his death, along with the deaths of their other companions. Because of the nature of his wounds, there was no doubt in their minds that Wilbarger was dead, and they cannot be blamed for their conclusions.

That night Mrs. Hornsby had a dream—a vivid, terrifying dream. She saw Wilbarger lying in the dirt beneath the scrub cedars, caked with blood, naked, scalped—but alive. She awoke, and decided she had only been having a nightmare. But when she went back to sleep and had the same dream again she aroused her husband and insisted that the men go look for Wilbarger.

They tried to explain to her that she was having such dreams because of the tragic experiences of the day before, but Mrs. Hornsby refused to be placated by their argument. At her insistence, the men started out early the next morning on a search which they knew would be fruitless. They carefully and cautiously searched the scene of the ambush for some time before they came upon Wilbarger's bloody trail and they found him propped up against a scrubby cedar stump, more dead than alive. The men carried him to the nearby stream, washed him and bound his wounds as best they could—and then wrapped him in blankets for the painful journey to the settlement.

Wilbarger recovered and lived for eleven years after his incredible brush with death. He had been rescued as the direct result of Mrs. Hornsby's vivid dreams.

Perhaps the most puzzling feature of the case, however, was that involving Wilbarger's sister, who had appeared to him under such strange circumstances.

The sister had died in Missouri just twenty-four hours before she appeared to the stricken man as he crawled along in that thicket in Texas.

43

Stranger in the Coffin

In September of 1956 the Kalabany brothers of Westport, Connecticut, were digging in the family burial plot in Green Farms Congregational Church Cemetery. There was room for one more burial in the plot —a spot where no member of the family had yet been interred. Imagine the astonishment of the brothers when they came upon a coffin—where no coffin should have been! And when they opened it they discovered that it contained the body of a man whom they had never seen before. He was a ruddy-cheeked fellow about forty-five to fifty years of age, dressed in an expensive blue suit which had been freshly pressed. He gave every indication of having been a man of substance and possibly of some importance, for the coffin in which he lay was one that had been rather expensive. The big question was—who was he and how did he get into that grave where no one was supposed to be buried?

Since he could not be identified, no permit could be issued to remove him; and the Kalabany brothers covered him again—reluctantly, of course. The following spring, after the irate brothers had pestered the cemetery authorities and the police about the stranger in their family burial plot, the police decided to investigate.

They dug up the same plot again. They found a coffin. But when they opened it they found only the skeleton of a man who had been dead at least fifty years, according to necrologists.

Both Harry and Henry Kalabany protested that this was not the coffin they had dug up a few months previously, nor was it the body they had found. The police could only shrug their shoulders and restore the skeleton to its purloined resting place.

Had the body the brothers found been that of a murder victim, hidden in this unlikely place and accidentally discovered? Had the slayer learned of the discovery and removed the body, replacing it with another? Or had it indeed been the same body, rapidly disintegrated after having been exposed to the air, as is sometimes known to happen?

Or, as some suspect, had the Kalabany brothers seen him as he used to be, rather than as he actually was when they found him?

The stranger in the Kalabany grave must remain there, said the law, until he is identified. Which may mean that he is going to be there for a long, long time!

44

Headlines in Advance

When the word got around, via the news wires, that Dr. Spencer Thornton was able to predict newspaper headlines days or weeks ahead of publication, naturally there were some skeptics. It was 1957, and Dr. Thornton, then twenty-nine years old, was reportedly beating the newspapers at their own game by describing in advance what the papers were going to be selling and telling. Well, was he . . . or was he not?

The Dallas, Texas, TIMES HERALD, decided to find out —and how better than by putting the young medic to the test? Would he dare?

Yes, he would.

Staff writer Paul Rosenfield met Dr. Thornton and asked him to submit proof of his alleged prowess as a prognosticator of newspaper headlines.

Dr. Thornton promptly scribbled down a few lines on a piece of paper and put it into an envelope addressed to Mr. Rosenfield at the newsaper. Rosenfield sealed the envelope and mailed it to himself.

After the letter was safely in the mailbox, Dr. Thornton told Rosenfield that he had answered three questions which he had not yet asked the newsman.

157

1. How much money was in Rosenfield's pockets?
   Dr. Thornton had written $4.45.
2. What was Rosenfield's home town?
   The doctor had written that it was Clarksville, Texas.
3. He asked Rosenfield to think of any number up to
   1,000. Rosenfield replied that he was thinking of 632.

When the newsman opened the letter at the TIMES HERALD next day he found that Dr. Thornton had written down, in advance, the correct answers to the last two questions and had missed the correct figure on the first question by just one cent.

45

The Grassless Grave

In the Welsh town of Montgomery, several hundred persons had gathered to witness the execution of an Englishman, young John Davies, who had been convicted of stealing a purse on the highway. Davies had few friends in that crowd, for the Welsh are a clannish people and they resented this young man who had been brought into their community to help a local widow run her flinty farm. Davies had been doing well at the task until he was attacked on the road by two local thugs who demanded his purse. He refused and a fight started. Davies was badly beaten and, to add insult to injury, his assailants took him to Welshpool and charged him with highway robbery. The two thugs testified against him and Davies heard himself sentenced to death on their testimony. He protested the obvious injustice of both the accusation and of the sentence, but in vain. On the scaffold, with only seconds to live, John Davies held up his right hand and again cried out his innocence. "I die," he said, "praying to God that He will let no grass grow on my grave and that He will so prove my innocence." Just then the hangman sprung the trap . . . and John Davies plunged into eternity.

His body was buried in the Montgomery parish church-yard, but it soon became apparent that his grave was different. All the others were covered with grass . . . but that of John Davies remained barren. People noticed this and talked. The embarrassed authorities had the grave covered with sod, which promptly withered. Then they sowed grass seed—but that failed to sprout. Davies was executed on September 6, 1821, and buried the same day. In 1851 the cemetery was remodeled, the graves were covered over with two feet of fresh soil, and grass seed was sown thickly. Within two weeks the former cemetery had become a beautiful lawn . . . all except the barren rectangle under which Davies was buried. More efforts were made to sod it and to fertilize it . . . but in vain. Finally the succession of vicars decided to let nature take its course . . and the barren grave of John Davies was fenced in and left un-touched. . . . It remains to this day a grassless testimony to the memory of a man who asked for it *to prove his innocence.*

The immense marble structure which houses the Field Natural History Museum is deservedly one of the show-places of Chicago. The museum is surrounded by smooth, well-kept green lawns—all except for one spot which is a patch of dead, bare ground. A patch of ground with a strange story behind it—or beneath it, perhaps.

In 1956, the resident curator of the Field Museum had an assistant who was working beside him in the unheated basement of the building. The day was unseasonably cool, even for late fall, but the assistant complained of being uncomfortably warm and he told the curator that he was going outside to cool off. He lay down on the grass and a few minutes later he suffered a heart attack.

Fortunately, the man recovered from the attack but, as late as the fall of 1962, six years after the incident, that particular spot on the lawn was barren, while grass grew all around it. Oddly, though the soil has been removed to a depth of two or three feet and replaced, no grass has grown in that particular spot. Each spring the grass sprouts there, only to wither and die in that one little area where the assistant suffered his heart attack.

According to science, it cannot happen.

Trouble is—it did.

When Orville and Wilbur Wright, a couple of bicycle repairmen, persisted in their efforts to fly in machines that were heavier than air they found themselves flying in the face of dogma. Their first successful flights at Kitty Hawk took place in December, 1903. But in January of 1906, the *Scientific American* published an editorial entitled: "The Wright Aeroplane and Its Fabled Performance." Said the editorial:

"If such sensational and tremendously important experiments are being conducted in a not very remote part of the country, on a subject which almost everybody feels is of the most profound interest, is it possible to believe that the enterprising American reporter, who, it is well known, comes down the chimney when the door is locked in his face—even if he has to scale a skyscraper to do so— would not have ascertained all about them and published it long ago?"

Science was ignoring the Wright Brothers who had then been making public flights for more than two years!

46

Strangers in World Skies

At widely separated points on the globe, there were two well documented and noteworthy sightings of Unidentified Flying Objects in May of 1962. Newspapers in Europe and South America reported the incidents fully. News services in the United States ignored them, for reasons known only to themselves.

In the last week of May, on a day of maximum visibility, an Irish International Airlines Viscount jet passenger liner was flying from Cork to Brussels. The plane was at 17,000 feet about 35 miles southeast of Bristol, England, ground speed 580 miles per hour. Veteran pilot Captain Gordon Pendleton spotted an object, coming toward his plane and beneath it.

All the crew members and some of the passengers saw the thing.

Captain Pendleton said in his report: "I have never seen anything like it in my thirty years of flying. It was about three thousand feet below me, approaching at about 500 miles per hour. It was brown, disc-shaped and had eight or ten antennalike projections around its rim. We alerted radar and they picked it up, but it suddenly darted up and away and we all lost it."

On May 24, 1962, the Argentine Air force disclosed that it was deeply concerned by two sightings in remote parts of that country. One case they reported concerned a wealthy woman who owned a large ranch. A disc-shaped craft landed near her home and she went out to get a close look at it. The official Argentine statement did not give details on what the woman reportedly saw, except to say that she suffered from shock and was flown by Air Force helicopter to the nearest hospital, where reporters were not permitted to interview her. The Argentine Air Force did say, however, that the spot where the object landed was marked by a circle of singed grass about eighteen feet in diameter.

The other Argentine incident occurred two days after the one just mentioned. Eighteen army men and three officers, building a bridge over a small stream in southeastern Argentina, reported watching a silvery disc-shaped thing which settled down in a meadow about two hundred yards from where they were working. They watched it from the cover of the trees for about twenty minutes before it again rose slowly to treetop level and then zipped away . . . another Unidentified Flying Object.

47

Images of Love and Hate

In Bucksport, Maine, there remains to this day a visible memento of the days when New England was in the throes of its witch-hunting frenzy.

With so many communities in those days persecuting people for allegedly being witches, Colonel Jonathan Buck, the founder of Bucksport, decided that his village should not be overlooked. Bucksport, declared the Colonel, would also prosecute its witches.

Since the popular conception of a witch was an old lady with a prominent chin and eccentric habits, it did not take the Colonel very long to select his first victim. She pleaded her innocence but the Colonel would have none of that. She had done the Devil's work, he trumpeted, and lying about it only magnified the crime. She must be tortured until she confessed.

When several hours of torture failed to elicit the confession he wanted, the Colonel tired of this cat-and-mouse business and ordered the hapless old soul executed.

She was conscious to the end and, with her last breath, she cursed the Colonel and his fellow fiends and declared that when he died his tombstone would bear the print of her foot as evidence that he had murdered an innocent woman.

Colonel Buck never forgot that threat and at the time of his death the heirs took particular pains to carry out his instructions that the tombstone be flawless and well surfaced—as he put it—"Unblemished and without flaws."

That was what he got, too, a very imposing monument which was placed at the head of his grave about two months after his death. It stood there, a snowy white stone that was outstanding for its size, as befitted the founder of the community and one of its wealthiest citizens.

The sexton was the first to note the change that took place. He summoned the minister and the minister called Buck's relatives. Sure enough, there was the faint outline of a woman's foot on Buck's tombstone. Each day it became plainer. The family called the stonemason and had him carefully scrape away the annoying reminder of the old lady who had died by Colonel Buck's hand.

When the footprint reappeared after a few weeks, the stone drew crowds of the curious, and the heirs of Buck had the stone removed and replaced with another. Their efforts were in vain, for the outline of a woman's foot soon became visible on the second stone and, when that happened, the heirs gave up.

The stone is there to this day—and the footprint is there, too—lasting reminders of a period of insanity in our early history and of the part that Colonel Buck played in it.

Robert L. Musgrove was a railroad engineer who died in a head-on collision with another train in 1904. He was buried in the cemetery of the Musgrove Chapel Methodist Church in Fayette County, Alabama.

At the time of his death, Musgrove was engaged to be married to a young lady from Amory, Mississippi. For months after his funeral the young girl made frequent visits to the grave, where she knelt in prayer for as much as an hour at a time. What finally became of her is unknown.

By 1960 the tombstone over Musgrove's grave had turned dark from its struggle with the elements. On the eight-foot-high shaft many persons noticed what appears to be the slowly developing image of a young woman. The image is considerably whiter than the darkened stone and by 1963 was sufficiently plain to be seen from the road that passes in front of the church.

The likeness is that of a young woman in a bridal gown. The hair style can be distinguished, as can the eyelashes. The hands, somewhat indistinct, appear to be holding something. Persons who are familiar with the case feel that the likeness is becoming more distinct with succeeding years. The curious may see the oddity for themselves by turning west on the Musgrove Chapel road about three miles south of Winfield, Alabama, on Highway 13.

The image on Robert Musgrove's tombstone appears to be a living reminder of a love that was lost, but not forgotten.

For more than fifty years the curious have pondered the case of the tombstone in an old cemetery at Williamston, North Carolina. It bears the name of James W. Huff and gives the date of his burial as October 13, 1901. The stone also bears the deeply etched outline of a horse's head, which is interesting in view of the circumstances surrounding Huff's death.

He was very fond of his horse and took excellent care of it. One evening he hitched it up to a light buggy and went for a drive. Next morning his battered body was found beside the overturned buggy at a lonely spot on a country road. The horse was missing and was never found.

About two months after Huff's burial a passer-by noticed the dim outline of the horse head on Huff's tombstone. Gradually the likeness became more pronounced and within a year it had reached its present clarity. There are no cracks in the stone to form that puzzling image and no scratches or marks. Just the dark outline of a horse's head which has withstood the work of sun and rain for more than half a century.

48

The Mystery of
Mr. Meehan

Thirty-eight-year-old Thomas P. Meehan was a handsome man, a very successful attorney who enjoyed a profitable private practice and who held a counsel's post with the California Employment Department. His office was in his home town of Concord, and on February 1, 1963, Mr. Meehan concluded a week of hearings on employment cases in Eureka and headed for home. He left Eureka about 2 P.M., after he complained that he believed he was taking the flu.

At a bar in Myers Flat he stopped for a drink and, while there, he phoned his wife and told her that he felt ill and would be late getting home. Mrs. Meehan advised him to stop at a motel instead of trying to drive when he did not feel well.

At about 4:45 that afternoon, Thomas Meehan checked in at the Forty Winks Motel at Redway, which is a couple of miles north of Garbersville. After making arrangements to spend the night there, he drove into Garbersville and went to the hospital, seeking a doctor. He told a nurse: "I feel like I'm dead!"

While the nurse was making some preliminary checks

on him, and before a doctor had examined him, Meehan vanished from the hospital. Time, about 6:45 P.M.

Mr. and Mrs. Marvin Martin, of Myers Flat, reported to the State Highway Patrol at 7 P.M. that they had just seen the tail lights of a speeding car on Highway 101 vanish, apparently into the roiling waters of Eel River. The State Police immediately dispatched a car to the scene.

At 8 P.M. Tom Meehan walked into the Forty Winks Motel again. He said to Chip Nunemaker, the owner: "Do I look like I'm dead? I feel like I have died and the whole world died with me!" Nunemaker noticed that Meehan's shoes and the lower three or four inches of his pants legs were wet and muddy. Meehan went on to his room.

A bell boy went to Meehan's room at 9:30 P.M. to tell him that a call he had placed to his wife in Concord could not be completed because a storm had disrupted service. The bell boy noticed that Meehan had changed into a black suit and white shirt.

At 10:45 P.M. Meehan's car was found in the Eel River. It was submerged up to the tail lamps, which were still burning. There was blood on top of the car and a trail of bloody footprints led up the bank and toward the highway, where they abruptly stopped. There was nobody in the submerged car. Police said it had gone into the river at high speed.

Meehan was not at the Forty Winks Motel, although his clothes were there, and his suitcase. The wet suit and shoes were not wet and showed no signs of having been mud-smeared the night before. Meehan had vanished.

He had disappeared on the night of February 1 and he was not seen again until February 20, when his body was found sixteen miles downriver from the spot where his car had plunged into the river.

An autopsy showed that he had drowned. His head had been gashed but the wound was superficial. Meehan had evidently survived the plunge into the river only to drown later.

The case presented the authorities with a puzzle which was not solved. If Meehan got up the bank to safety and then stumbled back into the river—how did the owner and bellboy at the motel see him later? How could he have gone back to the hotel and cleaned up—only to drown later in the river miles away?

The State Police did not doubt the identification of Meehan at the motel; for both the manager and bellboy saw and talked with him. But how Meehan could be in two places at the same time—dead in the river and alive at the motel—has not yet been determined.

49

Who Was First in America?

It is virtually a certainty that the Indians who inhabited North America at the time of Columbus were relative newcomers. There are many bits and pieces of evidence—none of it conclusive, unfortunately—which point to the existence of earlier cultures of considerable attainment and widespread distribution.

One such tantalizing specimen is the strange symbol on the top of Medicine Mountain, in the windswept Big Horn range in Wyoming. There is a circle of stones, seventy feet in diameter, carefully laid out in perfect geometric form. The stones are arranged to form twenty-eight spokes radiating from a hub twelve feet in diameter, with a seven-foot open space in the center. Around the wheel symbol are six huge stones which seem to have served as chairs, possibly for the high priests of the people who built this unique monument.

The Indians had no use for the wheel and no idea of how it got there, although they knew of its existence, of course. White men first became interested in the design in 1902, when S. C. Simms of the Field Museum in Chicago spent considerable time trying to unravel the mystery. He could only conclude that it was a religious symbol of some race that had existed there between 15,000 B.C. and 1000 B.C.

Unless the strange rock writings of the western mountains are the work of the same vanished race, the great stone wheel on the Big Horn mountain top may be the only surviving evidence of their passing.

An old issue of the SACRAMENTO BEE reports that a resident of Sacramento has a rock that is elaborately carved; and that other stones, some of them weighing up to eight hundred pounds each, have been found in hydraulic diggings [placer mines]. Some of them were washed out from places which had been hundreds of feet underground on the bank of what was once an ancient river, long before the last Ice Age, which was something more than 10,000 years ago.

The first white men to reach the Dakotas were startled to find a tribe of Indians called the Mandans, living in well-planned villages around which they had erected deep-set log stockades, unlike any other tribe in the New World. Furthermore, the Mandans were lighter-skinned than other North American natives and many of them are said to have had blue-grey eyes, in contrast to the dark brown eyes of the Indians. Whether they were descendants of a group of long lost Welsh explorers, as some suspect, can hardly be known; for the Mandans were annihilated by a smallpox epidemic—another gift of the white man.

In my book *Stranger Than Science* I have reported on the giant human remains of great antiquity which were dug up at Rancho Lompock, California; at Crittenden, Arizona (in 1891 in a stone sepulcher); and at Walkerton,

173

Indiana, where in 1925 a group of amateur "investigators" destroyed one of the most important finds of its kind. They dug into an "Indian mound" and unearthed the skeletons of eight prehistoric giants, ranging from eight to almost nine feet tall, all wearing substantial copper armor. Sad to relate, the evidence was scattered and lost.

That these ancient Americans should have been clad in copper armor is, in itself, not surprising. The copper mines operated by these earliest Americans extend for hundreds of miles along Lake Superior. They are in many ways extensive and remarkable for the engineering used in their construction. But they were certainly not Indian mines; for when the white men came, the Indians knew nothing of the copper mines or of their purpose. The *American Antiquarian* (Volume 25-258) says "There is no indication of any permanent settlement near these mines. Not a vestige of a dwelling, nor a skeleton, nor a bone has ever been found." Just the mines—and their impenetrable mystery.

Near Heavener, Oklahoma, there stands a tall slab of stone about ten feet high, ten feet long, and a foot in thickness. On one side of it is carved a line of characters which appear to be runic in origin. They were there when the first white men reached Oklahoma; and that would seem to indicate that they were there when the Indians arrived, too, for Indians certainly did not go around carving runic figures in solid stone. There remains, of course, the final determination of who DID carve those old Norse characters into that slab of stone on a remote Oklahoma hillside—and when—and why.

Mute evidence of an ancient civilization will also be found on a hilltop in North Salem, New Hampshire, in the form of twenty-two stone structures, most of them half-buried.

Since they do not fit into the accepted "scientific" theory of a continent populated only by bow-and-arrow savages, these stone ruins have been the subject of considerable controversy, some of it quite heated. Let it suffice to say that the physical evidence is sufficiently interesting without our engaging in the controversy.

There are faded stone carvings of a gazelle head and of a bull's head; double axes (surely an Old World importation); and there is a huge stone slab similar to the sacrificial altars. of many ancient civilizations. That slab weighs about four tons and it is provided with a drainage groove of the sort typical on sacrificial altars.

At the bottom of an ancient well which has been drained, investigators found a flight of stone steps leading downward, blocked by a cave-in of huge stones which had once been part of the side and ceiling of some sort of channel or tunnel.

The stone village at North Salem cries for expert study and calm analysis. Today it is a dramatic meeting of the very old and the very latest—for near the sacrificial altar is a snack bar.

It may be pure coincidence, of course, but in October, 1954, a remarkable coin was found near Buttons, North Carolina. It bore the numerals 1215—presumably a date. The characters on the coin appeared to be Arabic. The condition of the coin indicated that it had lain where it was found for a very long time. The question before us now is whether it arrived there before—or after—Columbus.

These anachronistic coins have cropped up several times to plague the scholars.

During September of 1833, workmen engaged in boring a well near Norfolk, Virginia, were surprised to see a bit of metal brought up by the auger. W. S. Forest, who reported on the find in *Historical Sketches of Virginia*, says it was an ancient coin, oval-shaped, about the size of an English shilling, and was stamped with figures representing hunters or warriors, "similar to ancient Roman characters."

In Sullivan County, Missouri, in 1879, a farmer found what turned out to be an ancient ritual mask made of iron and silver. Since it was far beyond the capabilities or customs of the known primitives of the region, it must be regarded as the product of some earlier and more advanced race. Who were they? What happened to them?

We do not know.

Into that same category of the unanswerable we must assign the pair of tiny silver crosses found in Georgia. Writing in the Smithsonian Report, 1881-619, C. C. Jones describes the crosses as skillfully made, each arm of the cross being of equal length. Most interesting is his description of the engraving on the crosses. Jones says the letters are IYNKICIDU. What that means has thus far eluded the scholars, who certainly were not aided by the fact that the letters "C" and "D" in the inscription are facing the wrong way—in other words, reversed!

A minister, the Reverend Mr. Gass, undertook the excavation of a prehistoric mound near Davenport, Illinois. His finds included several inscribed stone tablets, of which the *American Antiquarian* (15-173ff.) says that one of the tablets contained letters and numerals both "Roman and Arabic." The list includes the letters "O" and "F" and the Roman numeral VIII. Also removed from this same mound by the same investigator was a stone tablet with the letters "TFTOWNS" scattered over the face of the stone.

This enigma intrigued the President of the American Antiquarian Society to such an extent that he made the trip to the mounds himself and fought mosquitoes while he dug. Mr. Charles Harrison duly reported to the members of his society that he, too, had found baffling stone tablets in the mounds near Davenport, Illinois. They were, he said, inscribed with Roman numerals—including that ubiquitous figure VIII—and other characters which seemed to be of ancient Phoenician or Arabic nature, but not arranged in such a way as to convey any intelligible message at this late date.

Roman numerals in the prehistoric mounds, like Roman coins brought up by well drillers, constitute such unpardonable anachronisms that they are customarily dismissed with polite sniffs and hints of fraud. If it accomplishes nothing else, that tactic eliminates the need for the embarrassing admission that we don't know who lived here before the Indians.

In Bradley County, Tennessee, a farmer named J. H. Hooper was intrigued by the peculiar markings on a stone which he found on a hillside of his farm. After pondering this oddity for a while, he began to look for others, and was promptly rewarded; for his search produced several similar flat stones with alphabetical characters on them, and—says the Transcript of the New York Academy of Sciences, (ii-27)—his diggings unearthed a lengthy stone wall which had been buried for a very long time. Hooper carefully cleared away the earth and debris, and could make out many signs and numerals which he was unable to read.

His notification of local leaders led eventually to their apprising scientists of the discovery. Subsequent investigation disclosed that the wall contained more than eight hundred individual characters cut into the stone. There were moons and stars and geometrical designs. There were also recognizable likenesses of animals. And the New York Academy of Sciences report cautiously adds: "Accidental imitation of oriental alphabets are numerous." Since they did not know who had done the work in the first place, their decision that the inclusion of oriental characters was "accidental" merely adds one mystery to another.

The wall is there. The characters upon it are there.

And the characters were concealed behind a layer of cement!

Perhaps the cement, too, was "accidental."

Among the list of such annoying anachronisms you will also find the strangely misplaced object discovered by Elwood D. Hummel.

He was fishing along the Susquehanna River near his home at Winfield, Pennsylvania. Elwood was a fly fisherman and he frequently waded the shallows of the Susquehanna. One day he chanced to glance down in the clear water and, as he did so, he noticed a small flat stone which appeared to have some markings on it. He picked it up and recognized it as some kind of baked clay, covered with tiny figures which were unintelligible to him. Odd, but not important to him at the moment, so Elwood dropped it into the pocket of his fishing coat.

For thirty-seven years Mr. Hummel kept that curious little stone rattling around in his fishing gear. Then one day one of his grandchildren found it and began using it for a toy. The handling and wear polished the stone and made the markings more distinct. The youngsters asked what the markings meant—and their grandfather decided that it was time he learned the answer to that question for himself. So he sent it to the curator of the Field Museum in Chicago.

Experts there promptly identified and translated the odd little markings. They spelled out the details of a small loan made by an Assyrian merchant in Cappadocia about 1800 years before Christ.

But no expert could explain how that ancient tablet got into a river in Pennsylvania in 1921 A.D.

Included in the undated evidence of ancient man in America are the stone ruins on a ridge near Mt. Carbon, West Virginia.

Among the ruins are stone walls which once stood along the mountain top, evidently built by men who knew something of military strategy as well as stonemasonry. The walls had been placed in such a manner that they were easy to defend and they had been so well constructed that they have survived the ravages of countless centuries. Who built them and what became of the builders are questions

179

likely to go forever unanswered. As with similar walls in Georgia, they give us a dim glimpse of the long ago when an unknown race flourished, built, and vanished.

[Work on the West Virginia ruins in 1958 was under the direction of Dr. James H. Kellar, of the University of Georgia, who had done similar work on the Georgia ruins. While studying the ancient stone work on Armstrong Mountain, Dr. Kellar came upon one man-made device which he was able to identify. It was a moonshine still.]

50

He Flew
Through the Air

Is it possible for a human being to be suddenly transported over great distances almost instantaneously, without harm? Let us take a case from the official records of Mexico, a case which was never solved.

On the morning of October 25, 1593, on the Plaza before the Palace in Mexico City, the guard was being changed. In the bright sunshine one soldier stood out from the rest—and small wonder—for he was dressed in a resplendent costume that was quite unlike the others. He carried a different type of musket—and it was plain that he was confused.

When taken in for questioning he told the Mexican authorities: "My name is Gil Pérez. As to standing sentry here—why I am merely doing as nearly as possible what I was ordered to do. I was ordered this morning to mount Guard at the doors of the Governor's palace in Manila. I know very well *this* is not the Governor's palace—and evidently I am not in Manila. Why or how that may be I do not know. But here I am and this a Palace of some kind so I am doing my duty as nearly as possible." Then the soldier added: "Last night the Governor of the Phil-

181

ippines, His Excellency Don Gomez Pérez Dasmarinas, had his head cracked with an axe in the Moluccas and is dead of the blow."

The soldier was told that he was in Mexico City, thousands of miles from Manila, and he could not believe it. He was questioned by the Viceroy and his council, who were as baffled as the soldier himself. He was questioned by Church authorities and then jailed, still a riddle to all who became involved. Had he indeed been transported from Manila to Mexico City overnight—a physical impossibility in 1593? Was he a criminal, or an insane person, or just a chronic liar?

For two months Soldier Pérez languished in jail in Mexico City, until a ship arrived from the Philippines. It brought news that Governor Dasmarinas had indeed been murdered in the Moluccas . . . and other passengers not only identified Soldier Pérez but recalled seeing him in Manila the day before he was arrested in Mexico City. Unable to explain what had happened to the poor fellow, the authorities carefully recorded the facts and sent him back to Manila, then, as now, an unsolved enigma of space and time.

51

*Outdated Soviet
Discoveries*

Is it possible to revive a warm-blooded creature which has been frozen to death? It is certainly an intriguing topic, however illogical it may seem . . . and more has been done in that direction than is generally realized.

In February of 1963 the news wires carried reports that Soviet scientists had succeeded in reviving two salamanders that had been found, frozen stiff, in the tundra of Siberia. The reports were based on an article in the Soviet magazine *Neva* and related that Professor Gleb Lozinolozinski of the Leningrad Institute of Cytology was one of the scientists who were involved in the remarkable experiment. Cytology, incidentally, is a branch of biology dealing with the structure, life, and function of living cells.

According to the report, two of the salamanders known as Tritons were found frozen in Siberia, at a depth of 25 feet. They had presumably been dead about 5,000 years; but, when slowly thawed out at room temperature, one of them revived and lived about a week, the other

183

was reportedly still alive three weeks later when it was shipped to the Moscow University laboratories.

Professor Lozinolozinski subsequently denied the report, calling it untrue and unscientific. It may well have been untrue; but to call it unscientific is to forget the facts . . . for warm-blooded creatures *have* been revived after death by freezing . . . and it was done right here in the United States. On April 6, 1935, in Los Angeles, medical researcher Dr. Ralph Willard exhibited a tubercular rhesus monkey which had been frozen stiff for three days and then revived—one of several test animals to survive the freezing. Dr. Willard felt that freezing and reviving might benefit victims of tuberculosis. His story was carried by the newspapers, and volunteers flocked to offer themselves as test cases. He selected a young man who was the son of a Columbia University professor . . . to be frozen to death and then revived. But the authorities stepped in . . . and Dr. Willard went back to less dramatic forms of medical research. An American scientific first that has been largely forgotten.

52

Astronomers See Mystery Object

A front page headline story in the Melbourne, Australia, HERALD on May 30, 1963, reported the astonishing experience undergone by three prominent astronomers the previous night at two minutes before 7 P. M. The paper identified the group as Professor Bart Bok, 57, a world-famous authority on the Milky Way; Dr. H. Gollnow, senior astronomer at the Mt. Stroml Observatory near Canberra; and an assistant astronomer, Miss M. Mowat. The Melbourne headline says "Three Astronomers See Flying Saucer" and it calls the report— "The best authenticated so far."

The astronomers told newsmen that at 6:58 P.M. Canberra time they watched a brightly lighted object moving across the heavens. It was in view of the three professional observers for one minute. Orange-red in color, it traveled from west to east, slightly BELOW the light cloud cover that was in the area at the time. It was self-luminous and was *not* reflecting sunlight. Too fast for a balloon, too slow to have been a meteor, and leaving no visible trail, the thing went almost directly overhead at the observatory in its transit of the sky.

Was it a satellite? The astronomers checked the satellite charts and found that none of them were on a path that would have taken them over that area at that time nor on that course. Furthermore, said the scientists, this object was *under* the cloud cover, much too low for any satellite.

In concluding their report the astronomers made a peculiar observation: "Whatever it was," they said, "it was definitely man-made!"

This is utter nonsense. Since they did not know *what* it was or *where it came from* or *where it was going* they could not possibly have known *who made it.*

The astronomers checked with the Civil Aviation control center and were told that no planes were in the area at the time.

Next day the Royal Australian Air Force said the astronomers had seen three of their jets in formation!

And to think that the military would send jets into the commercial aircraft airspace without notifying the control center is preposterous.

The headline was probably correct—"Three Astronomers See Flying Saucer."

53

The Ghost Was Right

Mrs. Alice Warren was a real estate operator in New York in 1955, and she was in the process of purchasing an old house which seemed to be in good condition. She was in the house one day, looking it over. The carpenter who was going to give her an estimate on the remodeling she had in mind was late for their appointment and she sat down to wait in an old kitchen chair that stood in the big empty living room.

According to the report by Whitney Bolton in the PHILADELPHIA INQUIRER, Mrs. Warren had been sitting there only a few minutes when she was startled by the appearance of a man who had stepped into the room from the hall without making a sound. As he bowed courteously, Mrs. Warren noticed that he was dressed in the fashion of the early 1800's. Before she could make inquiry of him he said:

"My name is Dillman. You are about to buy a house which, if you will forgive my boldness on the subject, has hideous plumbing. It will cost you a fortune to replace it."

With that the man bowed, stepped back into the hall,

and by the time Mrs. Warren could rush to the door he was gone.

She called in a plumbing expert who examined the house carefully and confirmed the warning given by the strange visitor. To replace the plumbing would have cost at least $4,000, so Mrs. Warren abandoned the idea of buying the place.

Some time later, out of curiosity, she traced the records on that old house. Between 1798 and 1808 it had been owned by a man named John Dillman.

54

Nashville Poltergeist

The poltergeist phenomenon is rather common, but it is by no means well understood. Just how it operates remains a mystery, although violence of some sort is a common characteristic.

In October of 1962, there were several riotous weeks of poltergeist activity in the home of John Hawkins at 1627 Ninth Avenue in Nashville, Tennessee. Mrs. Hawkins first became aware that something unusual was afoot when she heard a knocking at the front door. She opened the door but there was nobody there. It happened again and she accused one of her children. All the youngsters denied being involved.

While they stood before her, the heavy knocking occurred again—and again there was no one at the door. This continued intermittently all day and, when Mrs. Hawkins told her husband about it that evening, he told her she was imagining things. But the pounding went on all night, ending shortly after daylight. When it began the second night, the family got guns—"and," said Mrs. Hawkins, "that's when my husband began to understand what I was talking about!"

It was only the beginning. The sharp hard knocks came

from all around the house, first the front door, then the side door, and then the back door—so hard the glass rattled. Sometimes the knocking started at dark and continued to five o'clock in the morning. Police were called and they posted men around the house. The pounding continued but the police couldn't see who or what was causing it.

Once when the rapping came from a window pane a friend of the family fired through the window . . . the rapping just transferred to another window pane nearby. Another time, twenty football players from North High School sat on the porch, but that didn't produce anything beneficial either—the knocking merely moved around the house.

For more than two months this continued. Said Mr. Hawkins: "It doesn't hurt any of us but we just can't get any sleep with all that pounding going on!"

In the Nashville case, as in virtually all other poltergeist cases, the phenomenon seems to require the presence of teen-age children in the affected house. Whatever it is that causes the disturbance, it operates independently of the children, as though they were merely the spark that touches it off.

55

Fateful Forecast

In Owensville, Indiana, the citizens were puzzled one winter morning to find a cryptic message painted in huge letters on the sidewalk in front of the public grade school. The message said simply:
"Remember Pearl Harbor!"
People commented on the message. But they never knew who put it there—or why. It was really nothing to get excited about at the time it occurred; for the infamous Japanese attack on Pearl Harbor never took place until two years later . . . to the day.

56

Dreams That Paid Off

For more than two years the engineers at the Jones and Laughlin Steel Company in Pittsburgh had been having trouble with a major switch on a 10-inch bar mill. They had spent a great deal of time and money on the problem. They had altered the switch eleven times—and still it did not work.

It remained for a roller named Ray Hammerstrom to provide the long-sought answer which had eluded the engineers. Ray didn't worry about it. He just had a dream one afternoon in August of 1955, and in that dream he saw clearly the design of a new switch to replace the one that was giving trouble. Ray's dream switch worked perfectly—and won him an award of $15,000 from the grateful company.

Margaret Moyat is an English artist and a very good one. She has painted hundreds of portraits during her career, but the one that stands out strongest in her memory is one for which she is best known—a portrait that has never been explained.

One morning in June of 1953 Miss Moyat awoke at her home in Eythorne, Kent, England, after a particularly vivid dream. Not only was the subject of the dream a rather striking individual but it was an elderly man whom she did not recall ever having seen before. He just stood there before her, smiling faintly, as though he expected her to do his portrait. The impression of this unusual dream was so strong that Miss Moyat felt compelled to paint the old fellow while the mental image was so clear. She promptly set to work and finished the painting in two days.

About two weeks after the incident, Miss Moyat had as guests two ladies who had lived in Eythorne for more than thirty years. When they saw the portrait of the dream sitter, they gasped in astonishment. They, and other long-time residents of the community, pronounced the portrait to be an unmistakable likeness of a former minister of Eythorne, a Mr. Hughes. They remembered him for his twinkling pale blue eyes and his flowing white beard, both of which were outstanding features of Miss Moyat's painting. Other persons who had known Mr. Hughes while he was serving as Baptist minister at Eythorne also viewed the portrait and all pronounced it a superb likeness.

It is interesting, and a bit baffling, to note that Miss Moyat had lived in Eythorne only two years at the time she painted the picture. She did not attend the Baptist church and had never heard of the Reverend Mr. Hughes. In fact, at the time she saw the strange old man in her dreams, Reverend Hughes had been dead for twenty-five years!

The new sedan was coming too fast to hold the road with that icy coating beneath the thin covering of snow. The Thioughnioga River was deep and swift, right beside the highway. Too late the woman at the wheel realized her peril. She gripped the wheel, hit the brakes, and tried frantically to turn the car away from the river. Its front wheels turned futilely on the glazed roadway. The heavy sedan spun about once, straightened—and then crashed through the flimsy barrier and plunged into the river to sink like a stone.

Twenty-three-year-old Mrs. Fred Cordray of Marathon, New York, never had a chance after the car began to skid on that morning of March 6, 1938. The story of her passing was left in the tire marks which had scraped the snow from the ice-covered highway.

For seven days the volunteer search parties probed the nearby river for her body—which was not in the car that had carried her to her death. Their efforts were in vain. The searchers finally decided that they might as well give up and wait for time and nature to solve their problem; for all of those who participated were under the impression that the swift current had carried the body away.

At that point a truck driver stepped forward with a suggestion. He identified himself as William Knapp. He told police that he did not know the victim, but he had twice seen her body in a singularly vivid and gruesome dream. The picture had been so unforgettable that Knapp felt that he could find the spot.

The officials in charge of the search were not very receptive to Knapp's proposal that they follow him along the river bank until he came to a spot he had seen in a dream. There was a strong likelihood that they would be the laughing stock of the community if this phase of the search fizzled, as they expected. Only a few searchers went with Knapp and it is quite possible that even they had strong reservations about the wisdom of the move. But there was a goodly crowd of the curious, as always, and they thronged around the truck driver as he trudged along through the dense underbrush along the stream.

Finally, Knapp stopped. He was two miles downstream from the place where the searchers had been working so diligently—and with such little success. Knapp pointed to two huge trees that hung out over the stream.

"There. Straight out between those two big trees. That's where I saw her body. About fifty feet out from the bank and between those two big trees, in the eddy."

The river was coated with thick ice at that point. The workers used ice saws and axes to hack out a hole in the ice some hundred feet long and four feet wide. Most of them later admitted they felt pretty foolish, for this spot was well off the main current where they estimated that the body would be found.

Less than one hour after they began to drag the spot Knapp had pointed out, Earl Gillett of Scott, New York, had located the body—thanks to a truck driver's dream.

Betty Fox was the wife of a poverty-stricken blacksmith in Shropshire, England, in 1892.

One morning she told her family that she had had a strange dream in which she watched men in outlandish costumes bury something beside a road. Although they turned and looked in her direction from time to time, they did not seem to be aware of her presence. She, in turn, was not close enough to see what it was that they were burying so hastily and so furtively.

As such, it wasn't much of a dream, but the description she gave of the men was that of ancient warriors in heavy metal helmets and knee-length skirts, carrying thick circular metal shields. But the next night she again dreamed that she was walking down that same paved road and again she saw the same group of ancient warriors hurrying away from the spot where they had been digging. By various landmarks, Betty thought she recognized the place as being on the road between Uckington and Wroxeter. Peering under the bush where the men had been digging, she saw a handful of coins scattered in the dirt. Then she awoke.

Once again she drew only guffaws from her family when she recounted her dream and all she could do was to maintain that what she was telling was what she had seen.

A few nights later Betty dreamed both of the previous sequences again. She saw the men hurry down the road to the bush, where two of them buried something while the other two stood watch. Then she saw them hasten from the scene, leaving a scattering of coins in the dirt where they had been digging.

When she awakened Betty did not invite another round of ridicule by recounting her dream—this time she decided to do something about it. She got a spade and trudged off down the road until she came to a spot which seemed to be the one she had seen in her dream. There was a big bush, similar to the one where the soldiers had been digging. Betty went to work with the spade, and on the fourth or fifth shovelful she brought up a handful of ancient gold coins. She dug on until she had uncovered a thick earthenware pot filled with gold and silver coins of a type she had never seen before. Betty tucked the heavy pot under her coat and lugged it home. When she explained where she got it, there was no ridicule awaiting her.

Now that they had the money, the Foxes realized that they might lose it through some legal mumbo-jumbo. They kept quiet about the strange find and decided on a course of action.

They had a wealthy neighbor named Oatley who was a coin collector. Mr. Fox cautiously approached Oatley with just one of the coins, pretending that he had found it while digging behind the blacksmith shop. Oatley instantly recognized it as of Roman origin and bought it from Fox. When he was finally told the true story of the remarkable find, after he had assured Betty and her husband that they would not have to surrender the coins, Oatley arranged for the sale of all the coins to a professional archeologist, Thomas Wright, who paid Betty Fox and her husband $4,000 for the treasure—a sum that well repaid her for heeding her dream.

Betty subsequently took Wright to the scene of the find and he in turn took other archeologists. The outcome of their work was that Betty Fox's dream not only made her wealthy but it also led to the ultimate discovery of the ancient city of Uriconium, a Roman settlement which had been lost for more than 1,500 years.

Equally strange and worthy of note was the experience which involved an Indiana farm wife, Mrs. Bertha Stone of Jefferson County. On the afternoon of June 10, 1951, she was taking her customary nap when she had a disturbing dream.

She seemed to be standing at one end of a big bridge, near a city which she did not recognize. A middle-aged woman, very plainly dressed in black, approached Mrs. Stone and said:

"I came to Abilene to jump in the river."

Then, while Mrs. Stone watched, the woman walked to the middle of the bridge, climbed over the rail and leaped. Mrs. Stone did not recognize the woman, and she seemed unable to make any move to prevent her carrying out her suicidal threat.

Had such a thing actually happened?

Mrs. Stone decided to make a quiet check on the slim chance that something of the sort might have taken place in life as it had in Mrs. Stone's strange dream. They found only two cities named Abilene: one in Kansas and the other in Texas. They sent letters to the Police Departments of both cities inquiring whether anyone had committed suicide there on June 10, 1951, and if so, who and how?

The reply from Abilene, Kansas, was negative. But the reply from the Texas city of the same name revealed that on the date in question, a woman had registered at the Wooten Hotel under the name of Mrs. Ruth Brown. She inquired the way to the nearest river. After depositing her shabby suitcase in the hotel room, the woman walked down the street to the bridge and jumped to her death.

just as Mrs. Stone had seen in her dream. The woman's clothing bore no identification marks, the name and address she gave at the hotel were both false. Her real identity was not established.

Who she was, where she came from, and why she jumped to her death remain unsolved mysteries, as does the manner in which Mrs. Stone watched the tragic leap in her dreams from a thousand miles away.

57

The All-Time Champion Is Death

Prize fighters are well aware that middleweight champions seemed doomed to short and tragic lives. The first middleweight champ was the original Jack Dempsey, the Nonpareil. Defeated by Bob Fitzsimmons, Dempsey went to live in Portland, Oregon. He wasted away and was dead in six months, aged thirty-two. Stanley Ketchel was shot to death by a farm hand in Conway, Missouri, aged twenty-three. Billy Papke lost his title and went to live in Newport, California. He killed his ex-wife and committed suicide with the same weapon. Harry Greb, one of the greatest fighters of all time, underwent some minor plastic surgery . . . and died of the after affects. Tiger Flowers, Greb's successor, went into a New York hospital for the removal of scar tissue, a simple operation. A few hours later, he was dead. Doctors said his chances of survival were at least a hundred thousand to one in his favor. Vince Dundee another great middleweight champion, died of the same disease that killed Lou Gehrig. And when French champ Marcel Cerdan lost the title to Jake La Motta he said, "I win the championship back or I die." It was a fateful utterance for a middleweight king. The plane that was bringing Cerdan back to this country crashed and killed everyone aboard.

58

Does Science Follow the Flying Saucers?

The world-wide phenomenon of the unidentified flying objects known as "flying saucers" constitutes one of the most fascinating stories of the century —and perhaps one of the most important in human history.

These objects, in various forms, have been seen since 1947 in every part of the world. They have been seen most frequently in the heavily industrialized areas. A study of their appearances shows that they made systematic flights from one important point to another, as though they were mapping, which they may have been.

By the time they had ceased to be seen in numbers, one thing about them was well known to those entrusted with the responsibility of analyzing their activities:

These strange craft, operating beyond the capabilities and control of any man-made devices, *had visited every important communications center, industrial center, and military installation on earth.*

When this interesting and potentially ominous pattern began to develop, the government of the United States issued strict orders to prevent military or government personnel from discussing the objects publicly and provided

202

stiff penalties for those who violated the restrictions. Commercial airlines cooperated with the government by ordering their personnel to refrain from mentioning such sightings in public. Airline sightings were to be dealt with only by written report to the company officials. In cases where the pilots did speak out in public, they generally recanted or became strangely silent on the subject, for reasons which can be easily surmised. In fact, I have a tape recording of a veteran airline pilot describing a strange object which paced his passenger plane. The pilot was subsequently silenced by the airline, which denied that he had ever made such a statement!

When the world-wide compilation of UFO sightings showed clearly that they were engaged in a program of organized surveillance of the earth, culminating in their three memorable appearances in force over Washington, D.C., the lid of censorship came down with a bang and, by and large, has remained down ever since.

By patiently assembling the bits of authoritative evidence which are gradually becoming more numerous and meaningful, it is possible to recognize the true nature of such procedures as the incredibly expensive space program in which we are engaged. Why the great urgency to reach the moon, which we are told is nothing more than a dead and arid orb that has sailed harmlessly around us since the beginning of time? Why the big rush to get there— NOW?

And for that matter, why are we engaged in this headlong risk of life and fortune to get to Mars, which we are told is nothing more than a great frozen desert in the sky?

There must be a reason—a compelling reason—for our frenzied activities in these directions. There is a reason, and little by little it is beginning to show through the curtain of censorship.

Dr. Carl Sagan, eminent astronomer at the University of California, is also adviser to the National Aeronautics and Space Administration; is a member of the National Academy of Sciences; and, *most important,* is a member of the Armed Forces Panel On Extraterrestial Life.

Speaking to a meeting of the American Rocket Society in the winter of 1962, Dr. Sagan said:

"The earth probably has been visited by intelligent beings representing an advanced civilization from outer space!"

And he added that these space visitors logically would have built and maintained a base on our moon, on the side which man cannot see.

In Decatur, Illinois, on January 9, 1963, Brigadier General John A. McDavid, Director of Communications-Electronics for the Joint Chiefs of Staff, Washington, D.C., spoke at the annual alumni assembly at Millikin University. The University Public Relations Office, with approval of the General, prepared and released to the news media a report of the speech:

"General McDavid said we must be prepared for the future. Our relation to other life in the universe is part of this future, for as the British interplanetary scientist and author, Dr. Arthur C. Clark believes, there can be little doubt we will ultimately come into contact out in space with races more intelligent than our own.' "

204

Does Science Follow the Flying Saucers?

"General McDavid added: 'Before long people may be forced to realize and accept as a fact that this earth is only an infinitesimal grain of sand in an infinite universe, that the human is one of many forms of life with which God is concerned and that others are far superior to us.' "

" 'And, if this is true,' he warned, '. . . our meeting with other types of existence in other places in the universe quite likely will increase the potential element of conflict rather than reduce it . . . this imposes . . . an even greater burden of leadership on your generation,' he told the students."

Is this the background information on which our costly space program is predicated? Is this WHY?

Let's look at the record.

On December 14, 1962, our Mariner space probe sailed past the planet Venus, beeping its findings back to earth. It was a magnificent milestone for science but a fantastically expensive triumph for the American taxpayer. That series of radio messages cost us more than fifteen million dollars per hour—about fifty million dollars all told. And Mariner was but one of many such experiments.

Beginning with our first satellite launching in February, 1958, we have launched (or tried to launch) more than fifty devices of various types: Explorers, Vanguards, Discoverers, Echoes, Telestars, Samos, Tiros, etc. There is still another type of satellite, devoted to photography alone, of which we have at least five in orbit, although their launchings never have been officially announced.

This means the American taxpayer has spent about *fifty billion dollars* on various space projects in the ten years between 1953 and 1963.

Why? What grave emergency *inspired* us to embark on this program?

At first we were told we must beat the Russians to the moon. Then we were told, more generally, that we must support the space program at any cost "to beat the Russians."

But our fifty-million-dollar Mariner shot past Venus can hardly be included in racing the Russians. There are no Russians on Venus.

If there is a real urgency for this frantic drive into space—and there must be—then we must look beyond the official statements for it. Especially as you will recall that after the Cuban crisis Assistant Defense Secretary Arthur Sylvester said that the government had a right to lie and to "generate news" if a matter of national security were involved.

Following World War II we began to read news of "flying saucers."

From 1947, when they first appeared, to the summer of 1952, reports on flying saucers were carried openly by the news services; newspapers front-paged many of the sightings.

But the lid of censorship came down with a sudden and dramatic bang in August, 1952. That was the month sixty-eight of these strange glowing objects were over Washington, D.C., all at one time—on the night of August 13. Although this event occurred less than a month after the discs had visited the nation's capital in smaller numbers, the August 13 incident was so well suppressed it was not even mentioned by the news services. However, the full story was carefully compiled in a document, published by the Civil Aeronautics Administration entitled: "A Preliminary Study of Unidentified Targets Observed on Air Traffic Control Radar." It shows the patterns the objects used in flight, specifies which commercial airliners they followed, and it describes them for the guidance of government personnel who might be confronted with similar experiences.

The lid of censorship is still on.

Since then, we have spent a fantastic amount of money trying to get out into space ourselves. And we still are pouring money into the project, in many directions, at a rate which threatens bankruptcy.

But we no longer are told we must do this to beat the Russians. Now it is being done in the name of Science—which is to the space program what religion was to the Crusades.

The first project to follow the appearance of the Unidentified Flying Objects was the many-nation rush to the Antarctic. Perhaps it was mere coincidence that Russia, Sweden, Norway, Canada, and the United States poured men, money, and materials into many projects which still are largely functioning in the Antarctic; that Argentina, Chile, Australia, France, Great Britain, and the United States all sent expeditions into the Antarctic in 1948. Russia and Sweden joined the rush a year later. This means that within a twenty-four-month period following the appearance of UFO's at the South Polar regions, more nations sent more men and ships and gear into that area than in all the preceding two hundred years!

At any rate, expeditions to the South Pole produced two very tangible developments: First, the motion-and-still-pictures of the disc-shaped objects which circled the ships under Chilean Commander Orrego; second, the realization that these objects presumably were entering our atmosphere at the polar regions for a good reason.

Did it mean there was some invisible obstacle out in space above our equator, as a few scientists had cautiously theorized early in this century?

At the time we had no way of knowing but, as soon as we were able to contrive rockets capable of reaching extreme altitudes with the necessary instruments, we directed our attention to answering the question.

On March 2, 1958, it was announced that two of our Explorer satellites had confirmed the existence of a belt of intense radiation circling the earth about six hundred miles out from the equator. This zone we now call the Van Allen belt. There is no such belt above either of our polar regions and the confirmation of its existence evidently came as a surprise to our scientists, for the NEW YORK TIMES quotes them as saying that the radiation was a thousand times more powerful than they had estimated.

When it appeared that the UFO's preferred to enter our atmosphere only at the poles, science began to examine space over our equator and found the radiation belt.

Coincidence?

After the skies of the earth were invaded by innumerable disc-shaped devices which seemed to defy gravity, Canada, the scene of so many UFO appearances, set up a project under Dr. Wilbur B. Smith. Canadian equipment was adequate, rather than elaborate. Dr. Smith was a distinguished electronics engineer and an authority on geomagnetics. He and his staff soon noted that whenever one of these UFO's came within range of their gear, there was a sharp disturbance of the earth's magnetic field in that area. In other words, there was gravitational distortion induced by some phase of the disc's operations.

Two years after the Canadian investigation began, Dr. Smith was in Washington to attend an international conference on broadcast wave-length problems. In an interview he said: "From the weight of evidence, I believe that the 'flying saucers' come from outer space. And I think their appearance is what suddenly increased your government's interest in space travel and an artificial satellite. Judging from your own operations I would say that your government is also vitally concerned with the secret of propulsion."

West Germany, which had been the scene of so many visits by the UFO's, including some reported landings, named the world-famous rocket and space-travel scientist, Professor Hermann Oberth, to head their probe. After three years of studying the information supplied by his own and other governments, the outspoken Oberth said at a news conference in 1954: "There is no doubt in my mind that these objects (UFO's) are interplanetary craft of some sort. I am confident they do not originate in our solar system, but they may use Mars or some other body for a way station. . . . It is also our conclusion that they are propelled by distorting or converting the gravitational field."

Shortly after he made this remarkable statement to newsmen at Frankfurt, Professor Oberth was flown to this country and placed under security regulations as a consultant to his former student, Dr. Wernher Von Braun, at

209

the Redstone Rocket Arsenal. These regulations prevented Oberth from making any more public statements until 1959, when he returned to Europe. As soon as he landed in Frankfurt he told newsmen there was a world-wide effort to learn how gravity could be put to use as a form of energy. And he added that he expected men would be traveling to the moon in electrically driven devices within five to ten years. The United States, said Professor Oberth, had made great progress in this field of research.

Dr. George Gamow, the eminent geophysicist of George Washington University, says: "There exists a profound similarity between Newton's law of universal gravity and Sir Humphrey Gilbert's law for the interaction of magnetic poles. And if one can shield electrical and magnetic forces, why can it not also be done with gravitational forces?"

It has been obvious from the outset of our space program that the chemical-reaction rocket is not the answer to space travel. Too much fuel is required to produce too little usable energy. But if, as many scientists believe, gravity can be converted into electrical energy it will be possible to travel anywhere in space at fantastic speeds. This seems to be precisely what UFO's are doing.

Can we duplicate their performance, as Canada's Dr. Wilbur Smith and Professor Hermann Oberth indicated we are trying to do?

Just what has been accomplished I do not know. I do know we have spent—are spending—vast sums of money and great amounts of time in gravity research.

At Dayton, Ohio, the Air Force has a multi-million dollar institution, built and operated especially for this purpose. Government contracts for additional millions have been let to various steel companies and other industrial research groups since as far back as 1955, and renewed year after year. By understanding the force that holds man to this earth we hope to project man into space.

This is still another branch of scientific research that has followed closely on the idea that the "flying saucers" already are utilizing gravity.

Our space effort can be described correctly as a "crash" program—one that is driving ahead at full speed regardless of cost. This ordinarily would indicate an emergency—which it may be—but not necessarily the type of emergency that is being sold to the public.

The appearance of the UFO's in all parts of our earth in the late 1940's and early 1950's apparently jolted our top level authorities into believing the earth was under well-planned and systematic scrutiny—by someone from somewhere.

Obviously we have no control over these craft and thus far we have been unable to match their performance.

One phase of this crash program was the construction of giant radio telescopes—long-range listening devices designed to eavesdrop on the universe in the hope of intercepting transmissions from sentient beings on distant worlds. Or in not-so-distant space craft?

Tesla and Marconi both reported strange, unintelligible signals in the early part of this century. Ohio State University reported to the American Astronomical Society in August, 1956, that it had recorded interesting radio signals from Venus.

Our first space probe, the Mariner, was directed to Venus.

Coincidence?

The moon has been the scene of some strange lights and sights in the past half-century, according to astronomers. It is spoken of as a logical space base for men venturing out from the earth to other planets, and so must be considered a logical base for incoming traffic as well. Extra-terrestrial beings conceivably would use the averted side of the moon, which is always hidden from us. Perhaps this explains why the Soviet's picture-taking Lunik, sent to the moon, devoted all its facilities to the far side of the moon and took not a single picture of the side where they expect to land their own first space travelers!

We have by no means dealt with all the scientific activities which have followed our observations of the ubiquitous Unidentified Flying Objects. But I think we have mentioned enough to show that there exists a most interesting relationship between them.

It is difficult to believe that our "crash" program is motivated by nothing more urgent than "scientific research." It hardly seems likely that after thousands of years we suddenly find ourselves desperately in need of knowing, for merely scientific reasons, the temperature of Venus and the depth of the dust, if any, on the moon.

It does seem that the entire space program, intentionally or otherwise, is a process of trying to duplicate the performance of the Unidentified Flying Objects and of trying to trace their presumed path across space.

Isn't there some other motivation, well hidden behind the screen of official deception to which the American public has been subjected in recent years, behind our "scientific" exploration of space?

Major Patrick Powers, one of the Army's top missile experts, said, "There may be life on other cosmic bodies that would resent our intrusion on the moon and move to force us off. To be prepared for this our space ships will have to be armed."

Does he speak only from the military man's natural bent, or does he have some information which leads him to worry in this direction?

General Douglas MacArthur, asked about the possibility of a third World War, is quoted in the NEW YORK TIMES on October 9, 1955, as saying, "The nations of the world will have to unite, for the next war will be an interplanetary war. The nations of the earth must some day make a common front against attack by people from other planets."

Seven years later, addressing the 1962 graduating class at West Point, General MacArthur returned to this grim theme. *NICAP Bulletin* for October-November quotes him as saying, "We deal now, not with things of this world alone, but with the illimitable distances and as yet unfathomed mysteries of the universe. We are reaching out for a new and boundless frontier. We speak in terms of harnessing the cosmic energy . . . of ultimate conflict between a united human race and the sinister forces of some other planetary galaxy; of such dreams and fantasies as to make life the most exciting of all times."

Is this the real motivation behind our space program? Do those in charge of it know something we don't know? Something they aren't telling us?

Or is it just one more coincidence in the series of strange coincidences so evident in our space program—in our frenzied effort to follow the flying saucers to the stars —and perhaps to disaster?

59

The Mena Mystery

Three miles east of Mena, Arkansas, on Ransom Road, Mr. and Mrs. Ed Shinn lived with their fifteen-year-old grandson, Charlie Shaeffer, in the fall of 1961. Although Mr. Shinn was in his seventies, he farmed every day and his grandson helped him. So far, so good, but strange things were happening at the five-room farmhouse and on December 2 the story broke into the open.

Mr. and Mrs. Shinn told neighbors and reporters that for months they had been plagued with furniture, books, and kitchen utensils sailing around inside the house. Mrs. Shinn said that once she looked up in time to see the family Bible sail slowly past her across the parlor . . . at a time when she was there by herself. Pillows were jerked from under the heads of the elderly farmer and his wife with such violence that the pillows flew against the wall.

A daughter-in-law told of witnessing some of the phenomena which included an empty coal bucket and some ears of corn that sailed directly toward her. Mrs. Shinn's brother, George Wittenberg, told of seeing a pencil and a can of dog food hovering momentarily in mid-air. A

215

neighbor, J. L. Ply, reportedly watched wooden matches flying off a shelf—sometimes singly—at other times by the dozens.

An odd feature of the whole performance was the slowness with which many of the objects reportedly moved—for no visible reason.

After the beleaguered grandfather finally told a local merchant of the phenomena . . . and after the merchant told the press . . . the Shinns were overrun with the curious. As many as a dozen strangers at a time came tramping through the house—until the grandson stepped forward and claimed that he . . . and he alone . . . had been causing all the disturbance.

That ended the public curiosity . . . but did it solve the riddle? Charles Albright, columnist for the ARKANSAS GAZETTE, who investigated, says the boy's confession solved nothing . . . for Albright notes that not even Charlie Shaeffer could make heavy objects float around the room —as the witnesses reported. He found the boy's confession convenient . . . but not convincing.

60

Ill-Starred David

When David Bierman of Centralia, Illinois, was six years old he fell from his bicycle, and it took six stitches to patch up the cut. At seven he climbed an apple tree, touched a power line and was knocked to the ground, badly burned. At eight he was struck on the head by a lump of coal, and more stitches were required. At nine he fell into a concrete mixer and suffered several deep gashes, which required more stitches. At thirteen a roller-skating accident hospitalized him again. Later that same year he was back in the hospital for removal of a chest tumor.

By the time he was seventeen, in 1961, David had come to the conclusion that he had outlived his bad luck. He said: "At last my luck has changed!"

He spoke too soon.

In October of 1961 he was involved in a motorcycle accident in which he lost his life.

61

The Vanishing Letter

The Bishop of Grosswarden, Monseigneur Joseph de Lanyi, was ordinarily a good sound sleeper, but on the night of June 27, 1914, he found that he was unaccountably restless. So he did the next best thing—he went into his library and prepared to spend the rest of the night reading.

The clock showed a few minutes past midnight on the morning of June 28 when he entered the library and, as the Bishop flicked on the reading lamp, he noticed a small note sheet edged in black, lying beside the lamp. He could not recall having seen it before. As he reached for it, he recognized the coat of arms of an archduke who had studied under him some years before.

The Bishop read the note and was quite agitated by the message it contained. Why had it not been called to his attention before? Why had it been carelessly placed on that reading table where he might not have noticed it for another day? The Bishop laid the letter down on the table where he had found it and rang for his servant.

A few minutes later the servant came stumbling into the room. When the Bishop pointed to the black-edged note in question . . . it was no longer there . . . nor could they find any trace of it.

The eminent cleric felt that perhaps he had been experiencing some sort of hallucination and admittedly a very strange one. He had recognized the coat of arms on the unsigned "letter" as that of his former pupil, now Archduke Ferdinand. Just for the record, Bishop de Lanyi decided to write down the message while it was still fresh in his mind.

On a sheet of his own note paper he wrote:

"Your Eminence. My wife and I have been the victims of a political crime. We commend ourselves to your prayers. Sarajevo. June 28, 1914. 4 A.M."

Ten hours after the Bishop scribbled down that cryptic message, Archduke Ferdinand and his wife were shot to death in the streets of Sarajevo—the first victims of World War I.

62

Bobby, the Wonder Boy

The twelve doctors stared at the boy in amazement—as they had every right to do. They had just written long and involved sentences on the blackboard and this child with the strange look in his eyes had, without pause and without error, read back to them what they had written. It was a remarkable performance for several reasons—for one . . . because they had written their statements in Latin, Spanish, French, German and Turkish. Secondly, because the boy who promptly read what they had written was twelve years old . . . but with the mentality of a four-year-old.

Bobby, as he is called, came to the Kentucky Children's Home at Lyndon, near Louisville, in 1957. At that time he was six years old and the doctors had classified him as functionally retarded . . . able only to walk, talk, and read . . . but unable to dress himself.

This child was, and still is, an enigma to the medics. When he was six years old he strolled into the office of Superintendent L. F. Boland, whose medical diploma, written in Latin, hung behind his desk. Bobby glanced at the diploma and read every word of it without a hitch. The startled Superintendent wrote a couple of German phrases on a sheet of paper; the astounding "retarded" child read them back to him without error.

When a visiting doctor from Turkey came to the institution at Lyndon and watched the boy go through his paces, the visitor stepped to the blackboard and wrote a 26-word sentence in Turkish. Bobby did not disappoint his audience. He read the sentence back without a flaw, as the amazed visitor admitted.

Authorities who examined the youngster's background find that he came from a very poor family in Louisville. He had suffered head damage when born by Caesarian section. Beyond that the doctors admit bafflement. Bobby shows the reading ability of a high school student . . . but scores zero in tests. In some respects he is a genius —in others, a retarded child of four or five. He reads five foreign languages fluently, but whether he understands them nobody knows. Bobby, the retarded boy . . . leaves the doctors wondering.

63

A Bolt from the Blue

There is no stranger true story on record than that of the sudden and dramatic manner in which a civil war was brought to an end in Nicaragua. The year was 1907 and, as so frequently happens in the Latin American lands, a military group was seeking to shoot its way into office.

The rebels were making considerable headway under the astute leadership of General Pablo Castilliano. He had ample weapons, plenty of money, and an excellent background of military training.

General Castilliano and his forces were within easy striking distance of complete victory. The government forces had been defeated twice in quick succession, many of the troops had deserted and others were ready to throw down their arms if it looked like the rebels were going to win again. Castilliano and his officers had their troops strategically placed along a ridge overlooking the enemy positions. The blow which should bring them victory was timed for daylight the next morning. General Castilliano bade his staff good night and retired to his tent to set down a record of the day's events in his diary. At about ten o'clock he blew out his candle and went to bed.

A few minutes later the camp was lighted up as if by a gigantic flare. A flaming mass was streaking down from the clear night sky—coming straight for the camp. The terrified guard outside the General's tent yelled and threw himself to the earth.

The fireball struck squarely into General Castilliano's tent with a roar like that of dynamite. It blasted out a pit ten feet deep and about fifteen feet in diameter. The General died instantly. His guard lived for two days, long enough to confirm that it had indeed been a fireball from the sky, just as the other sentries claimed. Their story was later found to be true when pieces of the shattered meteorite were found in the pit.

The General's dramatic and almost unprecedented death demoralized his troops. They took it as a sign that their cause was in disfavor in Heaven and the rebellion collapsed overnight. It remains to this day the only known case where a war was brought to an end by direct intervention of a celestial object.

64

The Haunted Library

A public library is about the last place one would expect a ghost—or even a ghostlike sound. But according to a report by Loretta Lambroussis, writing in the HOUSTON POST in mid-1961—something surpassing strange was afoot in the Houston Public Library.

Many persons have heard the unmistakable sound of a violin. Sometimes it is only a few notes that are heard; at other times the music runs through an entire tune. The volume rises and falls; the playing is by no means that of a master.

For a time it was suspected that pranksters were using pocket radios to annoy the library staff. But that idea had to be dismissed because no radio station broadcasts violin music exclusively—and certainly none of the poor quality that floats through the library. Then it was suggested that some hoaxer had recorded some violin music and was playing it back on a tiny tape recorder. Trouble with that one is that the fitful melodies are sometimes heard when there is no one present but the library staff.

Whether it has any connection with the subject has not been decided, but the HOUSTON POST notes that the former janitor of the institution lived in the library basement for years. After hours he was given to strolling through the building, scraping away on his violin. Sometimes he would sit for hours on the balcony, playing many of the tunes that are heard floating through the building today. The janitor is gone . . . but the music lingers on.

65

*Does Death
Give Warning?*

Some day science may discover that human beings have some method of mental communication in moments of great emotional stress—and, if they do, that might explain what happened to Fred Trusty of 96 Riverside Drive in Painesville, Ohio, near Cleveland, in the fall of 1958.

Fred, aged thirty at the time, was building some steps on a hill behind his house. For some unaccountable reason he had what he calls a "strange feeling"—he dropped his tools and looked out toward a pond near his home. There he saw the placid surface rippling with what appeared to be the motion of a muskrat at play. Nothing unusual about that, for there were plenty of muskrats around there. But when he started to turn back to his work he felt impelled to look again . . . and this time he saw a little boy's cap floating in those same ripples.

Trusty raced down the hill and plunged into the pond. Seconds later he found the child on the bottom of the pond and pulled him to the surface. It was Trusty's own two-year-old son, Paul. Artificial respiration brought the child back from the brink of death.

Does Death Give Warning?

There had been no cry of alarm—no warning of impending disaster—just that "strange feeling"—commonly called a hunch, which saved the little fellow's life.

On Sunday, October 2, 1955, Airman Lawrence Monk was visiting his parents, Mr. and Mrs. Richard Ryan of Sheboygan, Wisconsin. He confided to his mother that he had a feeling that death was near. So strong was this premonition of doom that he gave his mother his Bible and said to her: "I won't be needing this any more, Mom. You'll never see me again—but you'll hear about me."

His startled and worried parents were unable to elicit any more information from him—just that gloomy prediction. On that particular Sunday morning Mrs. Ryan and her son went to church later than usual and took communion together.

On the following Thursday, Lawrence Monk boarded a United Airlines plane at Willow Run airport, near Detroit, for a flight to his base in California. The big airliner crashed into a mountainside in Wyoming and sixty-six persons were killed.

One of them was Airman Lawrence Monk.

The gnawing fear that something was wrong with his seventy-year-old Uncle Eugene kept plaguing Eugene Bouvee, aged twenty-three, of Clio, Michigan. It was a February day of 1958 and there had been no news that the uncle was ill, but his nephew could not rid himself of the feeling of unrest.

The next day he phoned a neighbor of Uncle Eugene's and was assured that the old man was all right, healthy, and in the best of spirits. Even that did not quiet his fears so just an hour after the phone call the nephew decided to drive in to Flint and see for himself.

When he arrived at his uncle's home he found smoke seeping out around the front door, which was locked. Bouvee kicked the door down but was unable to enter the house because of the thick, rolling smoke. He burned himself slightly before he gave up and called the Fire Department. Two of the firemen who answered the call were overcome by the fumes as they sought to rescue the aged man.

They were too late.

Uncle Eugene was already dead on the bathroom floor.

66

Strange Precipitation

A few miles from Washington, D. C., lies Fairfax Court House, Virginia. The ALEXANDRIA GAZETTE reported that in December of 1855, Fairfax was the scene of a cold rain which quickly turned to snow . . . but not ordinary snow . . . for the next morning it looked like a field of black velvet. The snow was covered thickly with incalculable numbers of tiny black bugs, smaller than the head of a pin. Curious citizens found that the insects were alive but apparently numbed by the cold for, when taken indoors and warmed, they became very active. The editor of the Alexandria newspaper declared bluntly that he was baffled, which seems pardonable under the circumstances.

If so, he was certainly no more baffled than the publisher of the Napa, California, REPUBLICAN, who lived through one of the most bizarre experiences of its kind when that region, and especially the area around nearby Clear Lake, was blanketed with a shower of rock candy in the fall of 1857. Rocks, trees, houses, and fences were coated; and in some instances the coating was so heavy that it pulled leaves off the trees. The substance looked and felt and tasted like ordinary rock candy, as children and pets soon discovered. Naturalists hastened to assure the editor that it was "nothing more than the exudations of some insect," but the editor cited all the evidence to dispute that "explanation" which, he said, "is a mere theory to excuse their ignorance of Nature's wondrous workings."

Ten years after the great rock candy deluge at Napa, the NEW ORLEANS TIMES reported an unusual shower from Louisiana. It was in March of 1867, and the countryside was glistening white, from the mouth of the Red River to a point some sixty miles away and in a strip from three to five miles wide. The weather was chilly and the residents at first thought it was just a powdery snow, only to discover that they were being showered with salt. It was dry and powdery and of high quality—but where or how it came from its point of origin to end in this unique shower remains a mystery.

The telegraph operator at Ozark, Arkansas, broke in on the line one day in November, 1880, to inform his co-workers that something mighty strange was taking place where he was located. Thousands of stones, some of them weighing up to two pounds each, seemed to be popping out of the ground, while other thousands—evidently of pebble size—were unmistakably pelting down from the skies. No damage was done, other than to the composure of the excited residents of Ozark and the surrounding countryside.

Showers of mud, two of which were reported from Australia and New Zealand in 1960 and 1961, are generally explained as high-altitude encounters between dust storms and rain clouds. At least that has the virtue of plausibility and may in fact be the answer. In March of

Strange Precipitation

1879, a passenger train was forced to a crawl near Stone House, Nevada, according to the newspaper at Winnemucca. The fall was so heavy that the tracks were coated almost to the point that the wheels could secure no grip. Coaches and engine looked like they had been dragged through a mudhole. The deluge lasted almost an hour and was largely mud, with little actual rain.

On March 26, 1948, residents of Dayton, Ohio, found themselves drenched with a green rain. Automobiles, houses, clothing, and sidewalks were all stained with the tint. There were the usual experts offering explanations which explained nothing. The rain ceased, the colors faded, and the inexpert experts were forgotten.

Fantastic numbers of creatures called water lizards came streaming down on Sacramento, California, in August of 1870. The editor of the SACRAMENTO REPORTER hurried from place to place to see this wonder for himself and he reported that there could be no mistake about it—these myriads of living creatures ranging from two to eight inches long had indeed fallen upon the city in a heavy rain. He found them spread thickly on the roof of the Opera House, and the streets and sidewalks were slippery with them. A well-known local figure, Judge Spicer, was having a cellar dug at the time of the storm and hundreds of the creatures survived for days in the rain water that collected there.

In Butte County, California, the community of Helltown was pelted with catfish and freshwater perch on the afternoon of September 11, 1878. For details see the ALAMEDA ARGUS, which promptly sent representatives to ascertain for themselves if this had really happened—and they reported back that it had, indeed. With the return of warm weather to work its chemistry on the litter of dead fish, there could be little question.

In previous books I have reported at length on the grisliest showers of all—the falls of flesh and blood such as those at Los Nietos, California, and at Bath County, Kentucky.

The list does not end there, as we shall see.

In July of 1841, Dr. Troost, Professor of Chemistry at the University of Nashville, received from Dr. W. P. Sayle, a respected physician of Lebanon, Tennessee, a package containing some fragments of muscle tissue and adipose matter which, Dr. Sayle reported, had fallen on his farm under strange conditions.

"——from a rather small red cloud, the only cloud in the sky at the time, which was last Friday between 11 and 12 noon, and about five miles east of Lebanon. The flesh and blood and adipose matter fell over an area half a mile in length and about 75 yards wide. It fell on the tobacco leaves, where the blood trickled to earth."

Dr. Sayle estimated that several hundred pounds of meat and blood had fallen, altogether. What the learned gentleman at the University made of this phenomenon is not recorded.

Newspapers in Richmond, Virginia, record a similar oddity on Good Friday of 1850, on the farm of G. W. Bassett near Cloverlea, Virginia.

There again the fall seemed to be associated with the appearance of a small reddish cloud which passed over the plantation about 4 P.M. Overseer Charles Clark and several of Mr. Bassett's plantation hands found themselves being showered with drops of blood and pieces of fresh meat which appeared to have been cut or sliced into thin strips. They were able to identify muscle flesh, liver, lights, and a chunk which was apparently the bottom of a heart, though what kind of heart they had no idea. It should be noted that no birds were visible overhead—just that peculiar cloud—and when the cloud passed on the strange shower ceased.

The editor of the paper added that a similar fall had occurred on a plantation in Simpson County, North Carolina, on February 15th of that same year (1850) littering the ground over an area thirty feet wide and nine hundred feet long with fresh blood, brains, and scraps of internal organs which could be identified. At the Simpson County deluge, too, there was mention of that freakish red cloud, which shed flesh and blood instead of rain.

In the SAN FRANCISCO HERALD under date of July 24, 1851, you will find still another strange incident of this type.

At the Army station located in nearby Benicia, the troops on the drill ground stared in amazement as blood and thin slices of fresh meat showered upon them. Their officer put them to work collecting the material, which was turned over to the station surgeon, who preserved the specimens in alcohol. He is said to have noticed that the meat seemed to be cleanly sliced into pieces not more than an eighth of an inch in thickness—much of it even thinner. Around the outer edge of some of the meat was a rim of very short black bristles.

In this case there were no birds in the sky, no rain, and not even that ubiquitous red cloud. Just the fall of flesh and blood and the mystery that it created by its presence.

At this point it seems appropriate to touch upon two more strange offerings from the skies which are matters of record. One of them is the case of a Union Pacific passenger train which sped through a thunderstorm in 1960 and came out of it with a twelve-inch trout stuck in the headlight.

And there was the motorist who was driving near Alexandria, Virginia, on December 22, 1955—when a frozen catfish crashed down through the windshield of his car. Where it had been up there in the wintry skies that morning will never be known. The first thought was that it might have fallen from a plane. This seems unlikely. For one thing—catfish seldom ride planes. And even though airline food is not always epicurean, it is a known fact that no airline serves catfish, frozen or otherwise.

Which brings us to Mr. and Mrs. Basil McGee, of 1005 Woodland Drive, in Gastonia, North Carolina.

The McGees were watering the lawn one afternoon in October of 1958—a bright, warm autumnal afternoon with few clouds in the sky.

Mrs. McGee was leaning on her rake watching Mr. McGee work. As she watched, something glittering came tumbling down out of the sky and landed in the wet leaves among some flowers. She picked it up—lo! and behold—it was a nice shiny new two-franc French coin.

No planes overhead—nor any Frenchmen, either.

I checked to ascertain whether Mrs. McGee might have been humming "Pennies from Heaven" at the time of this incident.

I regret to report that she was not.

67

What Happened
to the Moon?

That is a question which astronomers have been putting to themselves for centuries, and with good reason. An examination of the lunar landscape by telescope presents the spectacle of some sort of vast battlefield, pockmarked with craters that look like immense shell holes. There is agreement that the craters are there—but no agreement as to how they got there.

Some of the moon pits are held to be volcanic craters, an opinion which was strengthened in 1959 when Soviet astronomers at Pulkovo reported an apparent eruption in the crater Alphonsus. Other markings on the lunar surface are of such vast extent (and of such shallow nature) that they seem to represent the impact centers of asteroids or of huge meteorites, which may be two ways of saying the same thing. As even a good pair of binoculars will show, there are literally thousands of these so-called "meteor-craters" on the side of the moon that is visible to us.

Which of these assumptions really explains the nature of the pockmarks on the moon: Are they volcanoes—or meteors?

Proponents of the volcanic theory are quick to point out

what they regard as the major weakness of the meteor theory. They ask: "If the moon was bombarded by such a swarm of huge meteors, then how could the nearby earth have escaped similar devastation?"

Frank Halstead, for twenty-five years curator of the University of Minnesota observatory at Duluth, thinks he has the answer to this age-old scientific riddle. He says:

"The earth and the moon underwent the same catastrophic bombardment at the same time. The evidence is all about us: We have simply failed to recognize it for what it really is!"

Halstead admits that his surprising conclusions were not arrived at until he had blundered through the same pitfalls and misconceptions which he feels misled so many of his colleagues.

"Like many of my contemporaries," he says, "I was baffled by the undeniable dissimilarity in the physical appearance of the earth and its relatively close neighbor. It did, indeed, seem impossible for the moon to have suffered such a catastrophic bombardment while the earth escaped with little, if any, of the same treatment from the same source. This was the stumbling block on which the supporters of the meteor-crater theory had long come to grief —and I was among them. We simply could not answer that very pertinent question."

During his twenty-five years as director of Darling Observatory at Duluth, Halstead found ample time to ponder this lunar riddle. He concluded that most of the craters were impact markings, veritable celestial shellholes where gigantic bodies from space had smashed into the lunar surface and splashed themselves over the supposedly airless landscape.

There was considerable scientific basis for sucn an assumption.

The astronomer Piazzi discovered, in 1801, the first asteroid, which he called Ceres—a great chunk of material about the size of England, orbiting the sun in the belt where scientists had calculated that a planet *should* exist—but does not.

Subsequent close scrutiny of that same orbital belt disclosed that it was cluttered with thousands of these huge chunks, or fragments, which we now call asteroids. To explain their presence, astronomers formulated the theory of a planet that had long ago been torn apart by some unknown force. Such a celestial cataclysm would have resulted in two predictable and understandable results: It would have left a shower of jagged fragments orbiting along the path of the shattered planet (the present asteroid belt) and it would have sent another shower of fragments, large and small, streaking toward the sun. Some of this sun-bound shower would likely have crashed into both the earth and the moon with terrible impact, leaving great scars to mark their impact points.

The asteroid belt is there.

The scars are there on the moon.

But the earth does not show such scars—or does it?

At that point Halstead admittedly found himself stumped. With the earth's greater mass and consequently greater gravitational attraction, it should have received a proportionately greater bombardment than the moon. But the evidence that was so plain on the lunar surface was missing on earth.

Some of the smaller fragments would conceivably have burned up in their passage through the relatively dense atmosphere of the earth; but the larger meteors, some the size of mountains, would have smashed through to the earth itself, just as they apparently struck the moon. But on earth no such markings were found.

After years of pondering this problem, says Halstead, and after arriving at that same frustrating roadblock time after time, it suddenly dawned on him that the answer had been there all the time.

"The evidence has been under our noses for centuries," says Halstead. "Perhaps I should say that the evidence has been under our *feet*—for we have been so busy staring at the pockmarked moon that we have ignored traces of a similar bombardment here on earth. The physical evidence indicates that the earth caught its share of that titanic barrage from outer space—a great swarm of fragments of unusual magnitude which we intercepted as they swept in toward the sun.

"Let us examine the logical evidence. The asteroids exist in a belt where the laws of celestial physics indicate that a planet *should* exist. Examination of the asteroids shows that they are mere fragments, torn violently from some larger body; for many of them are jagged in shape and some of the larger asteroids are rotating on their longer axis, indicative of their violent separation from the parent body. "It is generally accepted," says Mr. Halstead, "that certain immutable laws govern the structures of the universe and this leads us to believe that iron and nickel, the commonest components of the earth, also constitute the core stuff of other planets. When such a body exploded, the fragments would consist chiefly of iron and nickel if those fragments came from the interior of the body. Fragments of its outer shell would consist of its stony exterior. When these stony masses struck a relatively solid body such as the moon, they would splash about in precisely the form which we see in the so-called rays which extend in every direction from some of the moon craters. On the other hand, the metallic fragments would crash down and form the craters with high and jagged walls. Or if they came in at an acute angle they would cleave great gashes on the lunar landscape, which may explain certain markings of that type on the moon.

"We can be certain of one thing—the earth and the moon underwent *similar bombardment at the same time*. That time period must have been short and terrible. I say short because there are so many craters on the moon which are perfectly formed and undamaged, and this would not have been true had the bombardment been prolonged. This again supports the belief that the masses which struck were part of a larger body that had been suddenly and violently torn apart, hurling part of its mass toward the sun and into eventual collision with the earth and the moon.

"The key to the riddle of the moon markings is to be found in a study of time," says astronomer Halstead. "The earth and moon are part of the same solar system and were therefore of the same age. But the moon, being so much smaller than the earth, cooled much earlier and had become a solid body at a time while the earth was still in

239

a plastic state. When that great shower of meteoric masses struck the moon in that dim and distant age, they struck a firm surface and left visible evidence on that surface. When other fragments of that same celestial barrage struck the earth they collided with a body that was still relatively hot and viscid—the asteroids embedded themselves in its great bulk—like rocks dropping into semi-liquid tar. Absorbed, they were by no means obliterated. We now have the means of locating some of the larger masses."

The means to which Halstead refers include electronic devices which can be used on the surface or suspended from planes; and, since 1957, the use of still more delicate instruments circling the earth in satellites. For instance, Dr. Gordon F. McDonald of the National Aeronautics and Space Administration revealed in 1961 that our instrumented satellites have shown the presence of mountain-size lumps of unknown character and origin embedded in the earth at various depths up to several hundred miles. Halstead concludes that these lumps are in reality some of the more impressive meteors which struck the semi-plastic earth and are being absorbed by it. If they are great masses of iron, their presence would also explain several terrestial peculiarities, including the meanderings of the magnetic North Pole—and possibly some of the wobble in the axis of the earth itself.

Halstead says: "We must also remember that most of these masses were simply huge chunks of iron. Those of relatively small bulk would have remained on or near the surface of the earth; larger bodies coming in at an acute angle would have cut great gashes and left metallic deposits for miles. I think we can name some of them today as the Mesabi Iron Range in Minnesota, the Labrador Range in Canada, and the mountain of iron which is now being worked by American interests in Venezuela."

Chunks of metals from space, imbedding themselves in the earth's surface, would seem to explain many of the deposits now being mined all over the globe.

Halstead's theory has much to support it, but it has yet to find conclusive proof. When will that come?

He says:

"Man's forthcoming scientific expeditions to the moon should teach us a great deal about the history of our own planet by enabling us to study the well-preserved story of its traveling companion's experiences. I am firmly convinced that those studies on the moon will fully confirm my own theory that the great surface scars on the moon were created at the same time and by the same means as the great metal deposits *on* and *in* the outer shell of the earth. The smaller moon, having already hardened, simply shows the marks which the larger and hotter earth absorbed.

"The *evidence* of what happened is here on earth. The *proof* of what happened is there on the moon!"

68

Strange Journey

The long and distinguished career of Captain Edward Sabine is predicated largely on his work as an astronomer, of course, for it was in that field that most of his work was done. And it was as an astronomer that the Royal Institution sent him to Africa in 1822 to study the motions of the pendulum and to note especially its variations at different distances from the equator.

Thus it was that Captain Sabine happened to be on Cape Lopez that year, at which time he witnessed the destruction of a vessel laden with casks of palm oil. It broke up on a reef and the valuable cargo was swept out to sea by the strong current.

One year later, 1823, Captain Sabine was in Hammerfest, at the northern tip of Norway, again conducting his pendulum studies. To his profound amazement, the sea washed up at his feet the same cargo of palm oil which had been scattered from the wreck on Cape Lopez, Africa, twelve months before and more than 6000 miles away! It was incredible, but true, that he had been standing on the shore at the beginning and the end of that cargo's strange journey.

69

The Strange Death of
Lieutenant Sutton

According to the official U. S. Navy records, Lieutenant James Sutton was shot to death by his own hand in a quarrel with some of his fellow officers. He was a graduate of the Naval Academy at Annapolis and at the time of his death in 1907 he was billeted there awaiting assignment.

There was a dance at the Academy on Saturday, October 12, 1907, and shortly after the dance, so the Navy records say, young Sutton and two of his fellow officers got into a fight. They told the Investigators that Lieutenant Sutton threatened to kill them and went to his quarters to get a gun for that purpose. When he returned, they said, they tried to disarm him and in the scuffle several shots were fired without effect. Then, according to the testimony of the two surviving officers, Sutton put the gun to his head and committed suicide.

Young Sutton's parents lived in Portland, Oregon, and on that same fateful Saturday evening at about 8:30 P.M., Portland time, Sutton's mother had an alarming experience. She told James Sutton, Sr.: "I heard a terrible roaring sound and felt a smashing blow on my head. Then I felt stabbing pains in my body and my senses reeled. I don't know why—but I just know that something has happened to Jimmy—something terrible!"

The mother spent a sleepless night in tears and prayer, for the feeling that calamity had overtaken her boy was unshakeable. At 2:30 A.M. the phone rang and Mr. Sutton answered it. Without revealing the nature of the call, he left the house and returned about an hour later. He put his arms around his wife and told her to prepare for a shock. As gently as possible he broke the news: He had gone to pick up a telegram notifying them that Lieutenant Sutton was dead, shot to death by his own hand.

Mrs. Sutton said that hardly had her husband confirmed her premonition of tragedy than her son stood before her. In the account that she gave to Dr. James Hyslop and other interested parties, including her attorneys, the figure of her son told her that he had NOT committed suicide, but had been beaten with a gun butt and knocked senseless before the shot was fired. He told his mother that if she could only see his forehead she would see the marks of the beating. Furthermore, said the apparition, he hoped his parents would investigate and clear his name of suicide.

At this point the boy's mother asked his father and sister if they could see Jimmy or hear what he was saying. When they assured her that they could not she asked him to repeat it. He then said: "Mama, they beat me almost to death. I did not know I was shot until my soul went into eternity. They either knocked or struck me in the jaw, for there was a big lump on the left side. I never had a chance to defend myself!"

Then suddenly he was gone. But when a reporter for

the Portland paper came and told the parents that the boy had literally blown the top of his head off after a drunken fight, Mrs. Sutton says that Jimmy returned to her side and was right with her for four days, denying the newspaper reporter's account, as well as the report in the official Navy telegram which merely said that he had committed suicide. Repeatedly the apparition told Mrs. Sutton that he had been beaten and that his corpse bore the marks of the beating—and begged her to clear his name of suicide.

At the demand of attorneys hired by the Suttons, the Navy held a second inquest in July, 1908. Just what the second inquest consisted of is not clear, but the records indicate that it was largely a review of the first, with a repetition of the testimony by the same witnesses. This leaves one with the feeling that the Navy was more concerned with substantiating its original findings than with making any new ones.

In both inquests the reports stated that there was not a scratch on the face of Lieutenant Sutton other than the bullet wound. This was sworn to by three Navy doctors. Yet in the experience Mrs. Sutton had with her son's apparition in Portland, only a few minutes after his death in Annapolis, she says that he told her there was a bruise on his forehead and that there was a lump on his left jaw and that he had *not* shot himself.

These representations were in direct conflict with those made by the first Navy inquest and duplicated by the second. Which version was correct?

Mr. and Mrs. James Sutton refused to be placated by the conclusions of the second inquest and they demanded that their son's body be exhumed and examined by a qualified physician not connected with the Navy. After considerable delay, the Navy finally consented. The body was exhumed for examination in September of 1909, which was twenty-three months after Sutton's death.

The Suttons hired a Dr. Vaughan to make the examination. He found a large bruise on the left side of the lower jaw. He found a bruise on the forehead. He also found that the bullet which killed Sutton had entered the head above and behind the ear (almost on top of the head) and had plowed downward and forward into the sinus cavity, where he located a portion of the bullet itself. Because of the path of the bullet, Dr. Vaughan concluded that it would have been impossible for Sutton to have shot himself, as alleged.

In other words, the reports from the Navy inquests that there were no marks of a beating and that Sutton had died by his own hand were refuted by the evidence which was still plainly visible twenty-three months after the boy's death. Not only that, but yet another major discrepancy appeared. The Navy turned over to the Sutton family the gun with which their son had been shot to death. It was a .38 caliber weapon which had been manufactured when the victim was a boy of twelve. Actually, Lieutenant Sutton's own gun was a .32 caliber pistol which he had bought brand new. The bullet taken from his head at the necropsy was a .38. The Navy had produced the gun that killed Sutton—but it was NOT Sutton's gun as they claimed!

Dr. Vaughan's findings were damning to the Navy's official inquests in the case, of course. The conclusions of the Naval boards stood exposed as either deliberately fraudulent or woefully slipshod. Stung by the exposure, the Navy followed the traditional pattern of bureaucrats in similar cases. It refused to reconsider the case or to examine the body or the evidence. It closed the books and ignored the facts which contradicted its own findings.

The net result was that the death of Lieutenant Sutton has been allowed to stand in the records as a suicide. That it could not have been so seems indubitably clear.

It should be re-emphasized that, at the time when Mrs. Sutton claimed her son appeared and spoke to her in Portland, none of the other members of the family present could see or hear him. But certainly something very unusual was taking place, for Mrs. Sutton knew at that moment the conditions which existed in the body of her dead son, three thousand miles away. And everything which she described to the rest of the family that tragic Saturday night was confirmed in detail by the necropsy twenty-three months later.

Two major questions remain in connection with the strange death of Lieutenant James Sutton, Jr.:

Did an apparition of her son actually appear and speak to Mrs. Sutton?

If no appearance took place, how did she know what had happened to him and exactly how it had happened?

70

Curious Cloudbursts

Worcester, England, experienced a spring thunderstorm on May 28, 1881. The downpour began rather suddenly and many persons had to run for shelter. Those who did not reach shelter in time had a most unusual experience—they found themselves in a downpour studded with snails, hermit crabs, periwinkles, and still another type of crab which was unknown to those who examined the evidence.

The rain lasted for just under half an hour and, when it stopped, those who ventured out again found themselves treading on assorted seafood. There were millions of the marine creatures. They were falling from trees and sliding from rooftops and awnings. Cromer Gardens Road seemed to be the center of the phenomenon and witnesses reported that it was impossible to walk there without slipping and sliding. Since many of the creatures were edible, they were collected eagerly by thrifty housewives. Officials who investigated announced that the strange deluge had covered an area about a mile square—and the fall of crabs and snails was estimated to amount to "many tons" at the very least!

Now here, as in every case of this sort, the experts were standing by, awaiting call. First to be neard from was an unidentified "scholar" who assured the puzzled public that it was just another case where a waterspout had sucked up these creatures from the tidewaters fifty miles away and dumped them a short time later on the streets of Worcester.

The magazine for naturalists, *Land and Water,* found itself stymied when it came to accepting that "explanation." As the editor cautiously noted, it was a very strange waterspout indeed which carefully selected only four types of life from the score or more that abounded in the tide flats; furthermore, after picking out a few tons of snails, crabs, and periwinkles for redistribution, the educated waterspout had also rejected sand, gravel, shells, and seaweed which also abounded where it made its selection.

When the waterspout answer began to wilt under the light of logic, the local WORCESTER DAILY TIMES bravely rushed into the breach. The answer was quite simple, said the publication.

"It was the harmless prank of a fish peddler!"

Whether this was written with tongue in cheek or with foot in mouth may never be known. Also likely to remain unknown is the identity of this wealthy but profligate fish peddler who allegedly dumped at least half a million dollars worth of seafood (snails alone were selling at $4 a bushel!) on the streets of Worcester during that thirty-minute downpour in May of 1881.

While the seafood which showered upon Worcester was edible, at least, that much could not be said for the multitudes of four-inch eels which rained on Piacenza, Italy, in June of 1957. They were just a plain nuisance.

The nuisance category also claims the metallic foil

which showered the Penn Valley area near Philadelphia in the fall of 1957. Nice clear day and a great day for golfing until that foil began streaming down. Some of it was finely shredded—and some of it was in chunks the size of a man's hand. The Air Force denied that any of its planes were conducting experiments in the area which involved the use of metallic foil. But the stuff was there and it fell in such masses that several irate golfers at two clubs found themselves stymied by gobs of the metal on the putting greens.

A study of the records indicates that showers of frogs are considerably more common than is generally realized. On September 7, 1954, Leicester, Massachusetts, underwent a shower of frogs or toads of several varieties. For about a mile on Paxton Avenue, from Leicester Center to the Paxton line, the streets and lawns were alive with the creatures. Some parents awakened their children (for it was shortly after midnight) and the youngsters could scoop up buckets full of the tiny toads with their bare hands. The forthcoming "explanation" was that some pond had overflowed and washed the frogs into the streets. What pond it was they failed to specify, which is just as well; for subsequent investigation disclosed that the frogs were also to be found in gutters and on rooftops, an embarrassing phase of the phenomenon which did not coincide with the theory of the overflowing pond, of course. The truth may have lain nearer to an overflowing expert in that particular instance.

In October of 1912, William Bathlot was driving his mail wagon on a rural route in Beaver County, Oklahoma. He got caught in a prairie storm which was prefaced with dense black clouds and jagged lightning flashes. Mr. Bathlot buttoned up his slicker and the horse jogged down the road, for both of them were veterans of such encounters.

But this storm was different from any they had ever experienced.

A few moments after the first raindrops began to swirl about him, Bathlot heard a pronounced rattling in the wagon bed behind him. He thought it was hail—until he noticed that scores of tiny objects were bouncing off the back of his horse—objects that did not look like any hail he had ever seen. He stopped the horse and then he realized that he was watching the fall of a multitude of tiny toads, about thumbnail size. He could see that they were landing on their backs and that, after bouncing a couple of inches from the fall, they would jump to their feet apparently unhurt. When the shower was over Bathlot found hundreds of the little fellows among the mailbags in the wagon bed and, as far as he could see around him, the earth was alive with the tiny creatures. During the rain, he held out his hand and caught four of the little toads—none of which seemed injured by the experience.

Seafood on schedule is reported from Yoro, Honduras. According to newspaper accounts, the natives there have learned to anticipate a fall of fish each year at the beginning of the rainy season. When the big black clouds begin to pile up over Cerro el Mal Nombre northeast of town, the natives gather up pails and baskets and buckets and tubs and head for the grassy plains outside the town. Since Yoro is fifty miles from the coast and separated from it by a lofty mountain range, fresh fish is a rare treat. But that first big rainstorm of the season answers the need by showering down tens of thousands of sardinelike fish from three to four inches long in this grand-daddy of showers. It is an annual event that dates back so far it is lost in the mists of time, according to Honduran authorities who have investigated.

It was a pleasant September evening in 1960 when Mrs. Victor Mietens of 915 Holland Street in Saginaw, Michigan, stepped off the porch of her cottage onto the patio. Something thumped gently on top of her head. Mrs. Mietens grabbed for it and emitted a yelp of surprise; for her hand brought down a cold, clammy object, which she promptly dropped. There on the ground before her lay an eight-inch perch, still alive. Examination disclosed that it bore no marks to indicate that it had been borne aloft by some hawk. The perch was unscathed and unexplained.

The STANLEY NEWS AND PRESS of Stanley, North Carolina, is the source for the report of a phenomenon that occurred in the summer of 1961 at the home of Mr. and Mrs. Cecil Moose on Norwood Road, near that city.

There was a very ordinary rain shower, badly needed in the area. But after the downpour had stopped Mr. Moose walked out into his driveway and discovered that it was literally paved with tiny toads, each about the size of a dime. He and others who saw them estimated that there were thousands of the little fellows in his yard and in an adjoining field—about an acre of ground in all. On the following day they were still there and so thick it was impossible to walk *without* killing scores of them.

The usual local "experts" came up with the usual "explanation"—the toads, they claimed, had come from a nearby pond.

Since toads do not live in ponds (as frogs do) that one can be dismissed as invalid.

All of which brings us to the case of frogs from the sky—or should we say "toads from the tempest"?

The scene of this eerie deluge was Orlando, Florida, on the afternoon of September 26, 1953. The time, about 3:15 P.M. A rainstorm was in progress; not an unusual event in that area at that time of year. But this storm was different; for it not only rained rain, it also rained toads.

The three small daughters of J. S. Russell were playing in the yard when the rain began; and, before the girls could get to the front porch, they were pelted with tiny toads. That the toads came from the air was unmistakably evidenced when both the youngsters and their parents watched the little fellows bouncing on the hood and top of the family car, parked in the driveway beside the house. After the storm, the little girls picked up hundreds of the tiny creatures, toads so minute that they could easily sit on a dime.

Mr. Russell got the standard brush-off when he called to report the incident to the local paper. He was informed that the toads had probably come out of the ground. If this had been true, it would have constituted an amazing story in itself; for in that case the toads had "come out of the ground" with such velocity that they shot several feet into the air, landing on top of the automobile and sliding down the windshield while Mr. Russell sat inside the car and watched.

And that same night, in another rain storm, these alleged "high-velocity toads" again came pelting down by the thousands. This second crop seems to have been propelled with even more vigor than the afternoon toads, for the night crop included the roof of the house among their landing places.

Just how the tiny toads shot out of the ground so fast that they landed on top of the house, or even on top of the automobile, was not explained by the explainers. Nor, for that matter, how they fell from the sky if they did not rise from the ground.

There are some things which can best be "explained" in nebulous terms. Rainstorms of toads seem to fall into that category.

71

Mysteries from Another Epoch

Four uranium miners were working on an ore face in a cliff in a Utah mine. Charles North, Ted McFarland, Tom North, and Charles North, Jr., had hacked their way through the eight feet of sandstone until they had come to a fossilized tree in a bed of high-grade uranium ore. The only way they could break up the tree and get it out of the way was by blasting.

The explosion shattered the stony tree trunk—but it did more than that. It revealed a cavity in the fossilized wood—a smoothly rounded hole about the size of a hen's egg. In the cavity they found a tiny frog, shriveled and greyish brown, with long toes which were not webbed and with tiny suction cups on the ends of its fingers. The impression on the walls of the cavity indicated that the toad had once filled the cavity completely, but when found it was only about a third as large as the hole which held it.

The miners reported that the creature lived twenty-eight hours after being released from the stony sepulchre which had evidently held it for ages.

For added details see the Salt Lake City DESERET NEWS for February 2, 1958.

But there are no added details on the mummified seals found in volcanic caves on a mountaintop 2,500 feet above sea level in the Antarctic. Alaskan geologist Dr. Troy Pewe and his staff found eighty-one well-preserved seals, fifty miles from water, mummified by the perpetual cold of the Antarctic. How they got there, or why, will probably remain a mystery.

72

The Monster Apes of Oregon

On July 30, 1963, the Portland, Oregon, Journal reported: "Mystery Creature Seen Again in NW." The staff writer for the paper, Martin Clark, found the report to be another in the long series of such bizarre cases involving credible witnesses and incredible hairy giants.

In this particular case Clark described the witnesses as a Portland man and two women, including a married man and married woman who were not married to each other, and at their request he withheld their names from publication.

The incident occurred on a desolate stretch of highway between Satus Pass and Toppenish at about 1:30 on Sunday morning, July 28, 1963. The man was driving the car which also contained his two women companions and he had just passed another car when his headlights revealed a huge creature a few feet off the road on the left-hand side.

"At first," he told reporter Clark, "I thought it was a whitened tree stump but then I realized there are no tree stumps in that area. Then I saw that it was moving."

The three persons in the car agreed that it was a gigantic man-like creature nine or ten feet tall, covered with long hair that looked light gray in the car's headlights. They thought that the thing had risen from the ditch alongside the road and that it was loping away from the highway when their lights picked it up as they were passing the other car.

That report was quickly followed by others, including one from Mr. and Mrs. Martin Hennrich, of 3104 SE 66th Avenue in Portland. They told the paper that on Wednesday, July 24, 1963, at about 4:30 P.M., their boat was drifting down the Lewis River where they were fishing. Mrs. Hennrich said: "As we neared the Ridgefield (Washington) railroad bridge, I saw this object about ten or fifteen feet from the water's edge. It was about a hundred feet from us at the time. At first I thought it was a big tree trunk—but then it started to move. I thought I was going crazy when it began moving—loping away from us into the brush!"

The Hennrich's description of the thing they saw was that of a gigantic near-human or ape-like creature covered with brownish or beige-colored hair. The hair on the head hung down around the shoulders in a cape-like effect, as Mrs. Hennrich told the paper: "—like one of those hoods the Ku Kluxers used to wear. This thing was bigger than any human I have ever seen."

Year after year for almost a century, credible witnesses have reported encountering these hairy giants of the remote wilderness along the mountains of British Columbia and the American northwest. They were known to the

The Monster Apes of Oregon

Indians as "Sasquatch"—in recent years, after their immense footprints have been seen and photographed and preserved in plaster casts, they are generally referred to as 'Big Foot' reports. In most cases these creatures flee at the sight of man, but when they do not the encounters do not always end happily.

In 1924 a party of six miners was working a profitable little pit on the east slope of Mount St. Helens. One evening, according to the report in the LONGVIEW DAILY NEWS, the miners found themselves attacked by a howling pack of these giant hairy near-human brutes. The monsters threw clubs and rocks at the terrified miners. One miner, Marion Smith, told the sheriff of Cowlitz County that he had fired five shots from his revolver into one of the brutes at point blank range without knocking it down. All night long, said the miners, the giant beasts howled around their cabin, pelting it with rocks so big that they threatened to break down the door. At daybreak the miners bolted from their battered shack and, as they fled, the party found itself confronted by a huge hairy creature which they estimated to be at least seven feet tall, ape-like in appearance and covered with long, black or dark-brown hair. One of the miners shot the creature and it was seen to tumble over the rim of a crevasse which has since become known as Ape Canyon.

The terrified miners' report resulted in a search party from the sheriff's office, which found the battered cabin, with huge footprints impressed in the surrounding soil. The miners never went back to their claim.

In August of 1963 the OREGON JOURNAL assigned staff

writer Marge Davenport to investigate the area around the slopes of Mount St. Helens, from which so many of these reports of huge ape-like creatures had originated.

One of the first things she found was the newspaper report of the six terrified miners to which we have just referred. And what about the giant footprints? The Spirit Lake Ranger Station provided the paper with a good clear photograph of two huge near-human footprints which were found in a dry gulch two miles below Spirit Lake on October 30, 1930. The footprints are very similar to a bare human foot with five toes clearly imprinted. The feet measured 16 inches long and 6 inches wide and were estimated to have been made by a creature weighing in excess of 400 pounds.

One of the places visited by the Davenport party was the so-called Ape Canyon, of which we have previously made note. As they picked their way through the narrow brush-choked gorge, one of Mrs. Davenport's teen-age daughters discovered a footprint in some sharp glossy pumy that had dried and held the imprint. The footprint resembled that of a child—the mark of five prehensile toes showing plainly. Another of Mrs. Davenport's daughters, a forestry major at the University of Washington and thoroughly familiar with wild animal prints as a result of years of study, examined this specimen and pointed out that it could not have been a bear track.

There it was, a childlike footprint in an area where the sharp pumy would have badly lacerated a human foot. It had been made by some creature with feet toughened to that terrain—but what kind of creature?

The Monster Apes of Oregon

Bit by bit, cameras and credible witnesses are accumulating circumstantial evidence which may eventually help solve the riddle of Big Foot.

One of the favorite habitats of these weird monsters seems to be the lower reaches of the Lewis River, where Mr. and Mrs. Martin Hennrich reported seeing one of the giant brutes on July 24, 1963.

Their report was still known only to themselves when Charlie Erion, a logger and ranch owner who lives near the Lewis River, took his two teen-age boys for a walk along the river bank on Sunday, July 28.

Eleven-year-old Jimmy first spotted the giant tracks and yelled for his father. Mr. Erion took one look, grabbed the boys by the hands and hurried back to call a friend, Arland Brawner, a Portland businessman who was visiting nearby. Brawner brought his camera and made several excellent photographs of the immense tracks. Measured the footprints are 18 inches long and 8 inches wide. The creatures that made them had a stride of 4 to 6 feet and in order to have impressed them so deeply into the soil where they were found, was believed to weigh in excess of 700 pounds. Investigation showed that the tracks were clearly visible in the sand and mud below the tide line, as though the creature which had made them had been searching for food in the tide flats.

The Indians who originally inhabited this part of North America were not lacking in bravery but they were admittedly terrified by these giant creatures which they called Sasquatch. Down through the years white men, too, have learned that there are indeed, some sort of giant hairy creatures roaming those vast wildernesses—creatures which inspire awe and respect from those who see them—and ridicule from those who deny their existence.

Someday, perhaps, science may be able to take time off from the exploration of space to solve this documented enigma which is so much closer at hand.

There is more of man than the scalpel ever dissected, or even the microscope has ever beheld; and infinitely more of the exterior universe than any physical sense has yet discovered. There are countless myriads of stars that we never saw, and had it not been for powerful telescopes used only by a few, we should have had no knowledge of their existence.

—William Denton
Wellesley, Massachusetts, 1870

73

The Riddle of the Red Spot

Jupiter is not only the largest planet in our solar system but it is also one of the brightest. Even in a very modest little telescope it is visible as a disc with faint markings across it . . . and on nights when the air is clear and reasonably still you will see a spectacle unmatched anywhere else in our solar system . . . the famous red spot of Jupiter.

Because the planet is such a giant . . . with a diameter ten times that of the earth . . . it is logically the producer

263

of a gigantic display. That vast oval-shaped red marking stands out clearly against the rest of the planet. Scientists tell us that Jupiter is a great frozen mass, possibly frozen gases, lying under a cloud cover that consists almost entirely of substances which preclude the possibility of life . . . at least of life as we know it . . . which is something else again.

That Red Spot near Jupiter's icy equator covers an area of about two hundred million square miles, according to the gentlemen who profess to be able to measure such things. If their estimate is correct, it means that this single feature on Jupiter is larger than all the continents on the earth combined.

With such an atmosphere . . . what does that bright red spot consist of? Is it some kind of substance that has coagulated or some strange life form that is flourishing in that frigid atmosphere?

This question brings us to still another riddle regarding Jupiter. The principal marking on it—the largest of the red spots—has been clearly visible since 1949. The planet rotates every ten hours . . . but the Big Red Spot is not rotating. Therefore it has to be something in Jupiter's sky . . . an enormous red oval that remains fixed toward us, like an evil eye. It is another unsolved riddle of space. Perhaps when we are able to take photographs from a point outside the earth's atmosphere we will be able to find the answer to the biggest mystery of our biggest planet.

74

Mental Photographs

The wonderland of the human mind continues to produce results which science cannot explain. One such mind is that of a young man in Chicago ... Ted Serios. After a severe illness, he discovered that he has a unique ability to produce photographs of scenes that are hundreds of miles away.

In one test conducted in early 1963 in the home of Curtis Fuller, a publisher of Evanston, Illinois, Mr. Fuller loaded his Polaroid camera with a fresh roll of film which he had bought that day for the experiment. Mr. Serios leaned back in the big easy chair, held the camera at arm's length with the lens facing him, and relaxed for a minute or so. Then he carefully clicked the shutter and handed the camera back to his host.

Fuller and the other witnesses watched as the picture was developed and pulled from the camera. The finished picture showed an airplane hangar with the words "air division" clearly pictured ... along with fragments of other words which led those present to believe that it referred to Canadian Mounted Police. But what airport was it that this amazing man had photographed while sitting in a house in Evanston, Illinois? The picture was sent to the Canadian Mounted Police headquarters, where it was promptly identified as their hangar in Rockcliffe, Ontario. And Rockcliffe is several hundred miles from where Mr. Serio was sitting when the photograph was made.

He has done this sort of thing many times under test conditions which are designed to preclude any possibility of fraud or trickery. It would seem to be impossible, yet it happens time after time.

Sometimes the pictures are hazy . . . as though badly out of focus. Sometimes they are scenes within a few miles of the test point and readily recognizable to all present. But occasionally, as in the Evanston test, the picture will turn out to be very clear . . . and very far away. How is it done? The scientists don't know, the Polaroid Camera Company doesn't know . . . and Mr. Serio doesn't seem to know either.

PART THREE

I believe the "flying saucers" are
piloted by supernatural forms of life
who have observed earth for a long
time. I call these creatures Uraniden,
and I believe they are very intelligent
beings.

—Dr. Hermann Oberth
Father of Space Travel

75

Strange Companion

In Caracas, Venezuela, shortly after
6 P.M. on December 18, 1957, Dr. Luis Corrales of the
Communications Ministry took a photograph of the Soviet
Sputnik II. Since this was a short time exposure Sputnik
showed up as a short streak on the negative. Dr. Corrales
was surprised to find that Sputnik had a traveling companion, another streak that paralleled that of the Soviet
capsule. Furthermore this accompanying object jogged—
that is, it deviated from the path it had been pursuing and
then returned to it.

For technical reasons scientists who examined this plate
determined that the object photographed in flight alongside the Soviet Sputnik was not a star or a meteor nor was

it a man made object—for the change of direction and the return to the original path clearly showed that it was an intelligently directed craft or object of unknown type, which, during the period covered by that photographic exposure, was traveling in close proximity to the Soviet craft.

And later, in similar vein, came the findings of our own Spacetrack Center, known as the National Space Surveillance Center, published in *Newsweek* magazine in July of 1960.

At that time, Spacetrack's computations showed a total of eleven American and two Soviet objects in orbit. *Newsweek* also noted that many scientists were convinced that the official record overlooked at least one other space vehicle which was not of earthly origin.

Says *Newsweek*: "This satellite, they suspect, is a visitor sent by the beings of another star within our own Milky Way—a sort of United Stellar Organization perhaps—interested, for archeological and anthropological reasons, in how things are going in this part of the galactic neighborhood."

As far back as 1954, a West German scientific group investigating the Unidentified Flying Objects for that country's government, came to the conclusion that these objects did not originate in our solar system, but came here from some other galaxy. So the idea which *Newsweek* attributed to some of our Spacetrack scientists in 1957 was not new, but was still important and interesting.

The eminent Australian astrophysicist, Professor Ronald Bracewell, said in 1961 that in all probability another civilization searching for evidence of intelligent life in our part of the universe would send a space craft capable of picking up our broadcast signals and of sending them back to its distant base.

Oddly—or perhaps not so oddly—strange radio signals *have* been detected by our gear. Among the latest of these interceptions is that reported by a Norwegian scientist, G. F. Stormer. The signals he recorded are unintelligible to us, like those before them; but if we could decipher them they might easily explain such mysteries as the strange traveling companion of Sputnik II

76

The Picture in the Pail

From time to time I have reported the curious cases in which pictures—recognizable pictures —have appeared in unusual places and under impossible conditions. Some of these pictures were on (or *in*) plate glass . . . some were on window panes, evidently etched there by the alchemy of lightning flashes. To this list of incredible pictures let us add the case of the picture in the milk pail.

It first came to light in January of 1948, in Northamptonshire, England, when Mrs. Margaret Leatherland was milking her cows. She was somewhat startled to observe a familiar likeness grinning at her from the inside of the shiny pail, just above the milk line. The likeness, by the way, was that of her brother, Sir Robert Fossett, a famous circus entrepreneur.

All the members of Mrs. Leatherland's family saw the image and recognized it as the likeness of Sir Robert, whom they knew well. He never saw it, however, for within a month of its appearance in the pail he had been rushed to a hospital, where he died.

Meanwhile, Mrs. Leatherland tried to get rid of the picture by scouring the pail with strong solutions of soda

and even with mild acids; but, although the picture some
times seemed to fade, it promptly came back as bold and
clear as ever, in spite of her best efforts.

It was inevitable that such an oddity should eventually
appear in the papers, and this one did, in due time. Mrs.
Leatherland's youngsters told other youngsters . . . one of
them took a picture of the smiling face on the inside of
the milk bucket . . . and a newspaper published it after
verifying the story. The Northampton Society for Psy-
chical Research sent an official to see first-hand what was
going on . . . and, like those before and after him, he went
away baffled. Having known Sir Robert Fossett, he had no
difficulty recognizing the likeness at once.

To the dead man's sister the picture in the milk pail
became a thing of dread, which is understandable enough;
for several times when the bucket was two-thirds full she
would glance down and see the likeness of her deceased
brother . . . with only his eyes and forehead above the
milk. The experts were mystified . . . but what became
of the bucket is another mystery known only to Mrs.
Leatherland . . . who got tired of it all.

77

A Mark on the Moon

The more you study the moon, the more you will become aware that it is an orb of mystery —a great luminous cyclops that swings around the earth as though it were keeping a celestial eye on human affairs. Countless times trained observers have detected strange sights on the moon—lights, lines, ridges, domes, and geometrical patterns that seemed to be of intelligent design. To the thousands of such sights that have been recorded and forgotten, we can now add a very recent example.

On the night of November 26, 1956, astronomer Robert E. Curtiss of Alamogordo, New Mexico, was examining the lunar surface through his sixteen-inch Newtonian reflector telescope. Fortunately, he had a 35-millimeter Mitchell camera attached to the scope and was making test exposures on some new film. The Mitchell is a motion picture camera similar to those used by Hollywood studios and Mr. Curtiss was taking his test pictures of the moon at rates which varied from 24 to 48 frames per second at the time of this singular experience.

When he developed the film and made prints from it, he was surprised to discover that he had filmed an oddity of unmistakable clarity. It was a glaring white cross, located just to the northwest of the ring plain Fra Mauro, near the small dark crater named Parry.

Each arm of the cross was several miles long and the arms crossed each other at right angles in the center—that is to say—each arm of the cross was of equal length. Lying just at the edge of the shadowed section of the moon, the white cross stood out clearly—amazingly so. Mr. Curtiss submitted prints of his riddle to various astronomical authorities. Some admitted puzzlement. One asserted that there was nothing unusual about the formation . . . "just a case where two mountain ridges crossed each other at right angles."

Unfortunately for that explanation, it is physically impossible for mountain ridges to cross each other at right angles . . . and the mystery of the white cross on the moon remains unsolved.

You will find a picture of it at your local library in Harvard Observatory's *Sky and Telescope* magazine . . . for June, 1958, on page 414.

78

The Mystery of Little Margaret

In 1960, when Margaret Jackson of Sherwood, Tennessee, was only two years old, she suddenly became ill. The family doctor found it difficult to be sure of his diagnosis and, because the malady persisted, he took no chances. Other medics were called in to examine the child, but they too were baffled by the ailment. She was taken to Vanderbilt Hospital in Nashville and kept under observation for weeks. The illness, whatever it was, finally subsided and the little girl was returned to her home. She had recovered—but she was blind.

Her father, Johnny, is an electrician whose closest friend is the Reverend John Huske, pastor at the Episcopal Mission in Sherwood. Since the doctors had been unable to help the little girl, Reverend Huske advised the family to resort to prayer. For almost two years, Margaret and her parents prayed at least once each day for the return of her sight. There were times when they felt that it was all in vain and they despaired of the child ever recovering. But Reverend Huske kept urging them to continue the prayers and he prayed for little Margaret, too.

One night, almost two years after the first illness had

stricken the child, Margaret began to display the same symptoms again. Her terrified parents rushed her back to Vanderbilt Hospital without delay; for the physicians had warned them not to waste time in case of a recurrence. Again the little girl, now four years old, underwent interminable tests and again the disease eluded analysis. The symptoms subsided and her parents were permitted to take her back home . . . well once more but still blind.

One night after the evening meal, her father struck a match to light a cigarette. Margaret giggled and grabbed for the flame. Gradually, over a period of weeks, her sight returned as mysteriously as it had vanished two years before. She was able to romp and play with other young-sters once more—didn't even need glasses. Said the Reverend Huske: "Margaret is a living miracle—proof of the power of prayer."

79

African Manna

Starvation was no stranger to the tribes of Central Angola in West Africa. One tribe, known as the Seles, had lived at the whim of nature for centuries. When the rains came at the right time, the Seles had good crops and plenty of food. But when the drought came, as frequently happened, they saw the countryside wither in the searing sunshine, and both man and beast suffered.

That was the case in March of 1939. For months there had been no rainfall. The rivers were dusty ditches. The game animals had fled or died. The birds were gone. The crops had shriveled and even the grasshoppers did not bother to devastate the land. Some four hundred members of the Seles tribe were facing starvation, after more than a hundred of the very old and very young had already expired.

A Christian mission had been established among the tribe, and it was presided over by Carlos Sequesque. He and his family faced disaster along with the Seles, for they had no way to flee across the barren countryside.

One morning Sequesque missed his five-year-old daughter, Rita. Fearing that she had wandered off into the brush, the whole tribe turned out to search for her. Before the search parties could get under way, the child came into the village, eating something from a wooden bowl she carried. When her father inquired what it was, the child replied that it was manna, "like Moses ate." She led the starving villagers to a bush-covered area a couple of hundred yards away. There they found every bush, and even the earth, thickly covered with a honey-like substance that was edible. Moreover, it was renewed every night over that one patch, about half an acre in extent.

The child could only explain that she had been hungry and she had prayed for something to eat—like Moses had. How she had managed to find it in that remote brush patch was never explained . . . but there it was, day after day, and the whole village lived on it until the rains came again.

The Reverend E. L. Cardy of Capetown took a jar of

the substance to Capetown for examination. He was told
that it was some kind of honey—but how it got on those
bushes in such quantities nobody knows.

80

Weight Loss in Space

One of the most astounding discoveries in many years has gone virtually unnoticed—the discovery that objects in space may become virtually weightless. This is contrary to all scientific belief and expectation—yet it is true—and has been officially confirmed by an Air Force statement of November, 1960.

You remember, of course, the efforts to recover our Discoverer-type satellites from the air over the Pacific by snatching their parachute lines with special aircraft gear. Imagine the surprise of the scientists when they recovered a Discoverer, undamaged, and put it on the scales. The satellite had weighed 300 pounds when it had been launched into Polar orbit a few days before. But the scales showed that it had lost more than half its weight while in orbit; it had dropped from 300 pounds at take-off to a mere 125 pounds at recovery.

This was fantastic . . it was scientifically impossible . . . but there it was—a riddle to which science has no answer. And, furthermore, the satellite continued to lose weight slowly for several days after it was recovered.

Actually, the strange story of gravity gone wild began on Labor Day of 1960, when Professor R. L. Brown, head of the science department of Southern Connecticut State College, was called to examine some debris from a fire. An apartment house had burned, and in the embers fire officials found some chunks of metal fused together. They had been subjected to great heat and they were extremely light in weight. Dr. Brown examined the fragments and announced that they were portions of Soviet Sputnik 4, which exploded in orbit when its retro-rocket malfunctioned. But there was more to come, for on September 14, 1960, more metal fragments fell into the lawn of a private home in Woodbridge. One piece was about the size of a man's forefinger. It was coated with an alloy and was surprisingly light. Tests showed that the metal had been subjected to intense radiation, that it had lost more than half its normal weight . . . and that the jar in which it was placed was also losing weight.

This evidence is contrary to all we know about gravity . . . but it may unlock for us the key to gravity itself.

81

Murder by Proxy

In the autumn of 1921, Dr. O. A. Ostby and a group of his friends were holding a seance in Minneapolis, an occasion at which Dr. Ostby was acting as the medium.

He told the group that a young girl was standing beside him, sobbing, requesting those present to do her a favor. She explained that she wanted someone to write to the Chief of Police in St. Louis to verify that a girl had been murdered there some months before—a girl named Edna Ellis. When the medium asked why she wanted this done, the tearful spectre said she wanted to get word to her parents that she had actually been murdered—and that she had not run away to lead a life of shame as they had been led to believe.

On the day following this seance, Dr. Ostby wrote to the Police Department of St. Louis and made inquiry as requested. He received a prompt reply, signed by Martin Obrien, who was then police chief in St. Louis. Obrien confirmed that Edna Ellis had been murdered in November of 1920 and that her sweetheart, Albert Ellis, had been convicted and was serving a life sentence at Missouri State Penitentiary for the crime.

At the next sitting by Dr. Ostby and his friends, the young lady again appeared to the medium and thanked them for their assistance. She asked them to send the letter from the Police Chief to her parents in South Dakota, so they would know what had become of her.

Dr. Ostby noted that she had referred to her sweetheart as George Ellis, whereas the Police Department letter referred to him as *Albert* Ellis. The young girl replied, through Dr. Ostby, that her killer's full name was George Albert but she always called him George, although he was convicted under the name of Albert. Subsequent investigation confirmed that statement, too.

About a year after this incident, in November of 1922, the Supreme Court of Missouri reviewed the case of Albert Ellis and ruled that he had been unjustly convicted. He was ordered released from prison at once.

Dr. Ostby and his friends continued to hold their experimental meetings from time to time . . . and thus it was that on July 16, 1928, they heard again from the spectral Edna Ellis. She said that George was with her—and they were happy together..

Later investigation disclosed that George Albert Ellis had died in an accident in 1926, four years after his release from prison.

82

Where Was Bill McDonald?

Few courts have ever been presented with a knottier question than that which confronted a New York City jury on July 8, 1896.

The defendant was William McDonald, charged with burglary, which he vehemently denied. The prosecution brought forth six witnesses who testified that they had surprised the defendant in a house on Second Avenue where he was unmistakably engaged in sacking up articles which could easily be disposed of at a profit. When the witnesses came upon him, the burglar dropped the bag of loot, put up a fight and escaped—but not until all six of the witnesses got a good look at him. Without hesitation all of them pointed the finger at William McDonald as the guilty party.

Up to this point it was nothing more than a routine breaking-and-entering case, a type with which our police courts are all too well supplied. But the defense had a surprise for the prosecution—one which would make history of a sort.

As the first witness for the defense there was sworn in a distinguished looking gentleman who identified himself as Professor Wein. His business? Hypnotist! But it developed that here was no ordinary practitioner of the art of mesmerism, for evidence was introduced which made it clear that Professor Wein was an eminent medical doctor whose articles appeared in authoritative publications. He enjoyed performing hypnotic experiments in public and it was customary for him to take a couple of brief vacations each year for that purpose. Thus it was that Dr. Wein had been engaged in hypnotizing a man on the stage of a Brooklyn theatre at the precise moment that the crime of which McDonald was accused was taking place several miles away.

So far the testimony was a bit unusual for a burglary trial but only because of the nature of the defense witness.

Then the defense attorney dropped the other shoe.

He established that several hundred people were in the theatre during that particular performance and that they were watching a man being hypnotized in the center of a fully-lighted stage. Then the attorney asked:

"Professor Wein, can you identify the man whom you were hypnotizing at that moment?"

Professor Wein calmly pointed to the defendant.

"That is he. I remember him quite well."

A buzz of excitement ran through the courtroom and the judge rapped for order. The doctor's testimony was in apparent contradiction to the testimony of those who had struggled with the burglar. Was the doctor mistaken in his identification of McDonald?

Wein testified that he remembered McDonald well because the defendant had proved to be one of the best subjects the hypnotist had encountered in his long experience in the field.

But was that subject really McDonald?

The defense brought to the witness stand six citizens of Brooklyn who had served on the stage as a committee for the theatre management during Professor Wein's engagement. All of them identified McDonald as the subject who was in hypnotic trance in Brooklyn at the time of the attempted burglary in Manhattan, about five miles distant.

Was such a thing possible?

Professor Wein testified that while McDonald was in trance the subject had carried out the various suggestions given to him by the hypnotist. None of the suggestions included a trip to New York nor the commission of any criminal act. Said Wein:

"He was an exceptionally good subject, very responsive and quick to execute the instructions. I considered him to be in a cataleptic state—that is, deprived for a certain time of all sensations other than those I imposed on his will."

"Was it possible, in your opinion, Professor, for this man's spirit, shall we say, to wander while his physical body was in full view of the audience on that stage, in hypnotic trance?"

"Yes. Quite possible."

The jury had heard six witnesses who testified that William McDonald fought with them and escaped from the scene of an attempted burglary—at the very moment when Professor Wein and six other witnesses testified that the same William McDonald was in deep hypnotic trance on a theatre stage five miles from the scene of the crime.

The jury decided that all the witnesses were correct—that McDonald was being tried both body and soul. He was acquitted.

It was a case which is unique, principally because the judgment involved acceptance of the reality of a type of psychic phenomenon virtually unheard of in courtroom procedures.

There are several well-attested cases where an individual seems to have been in two widely separated places simultaneously.

In the eighteenth century, Arienzo, Italy, was a full four days' journey from Rome. On September 21, 1774, a prominent Neapolitan cleric named Alphonsus Ligouri was putting on his garments preparatory to conducting a community mass. Suddenly he felt weak and dizzy. He stumbled to a chair and slumped down—and fell into what appears to have been a cataleptic sleep.

Ligouri remained in this condition for several hours, during which the personnel of the monastery carried him to bed. When he awakened it was late afternoon and he was quite surprised to find himself in bed, with the priests and domestics of the monastery gathered about him.

They explained that they had feared that he was dead or dying.

"Not at all," said Monsignor Ligouri, "but I have just come from the bedside of the Pope in Rome He is now dead!"

Those at the bedside assumed that Ligouri was simply

accepting a vivid dream as fact. Many of them regarded it as mere coincidence when word came from Rome, four days later, that the Pope had indeed died at the time Ligouri had stated—and while Ligouri was in his cataleptic condition in Arienzo.

The mystery was only deepened when the official reports of the Pope's death reached Arienzo, for among those who had prayed at the bedside of the dying pontiff was Alphonsus Ligouri! Subsequent investigation confirmed that many of those present on that occasion had talked with him and there could be no doubt about the identification.

Alphonsus Ligouri was in a cataleptic condition in Arienzo and was kneeling in prayer beside the Pope's bed in Rome at the same time, according to scores of credible witnesses.

It was another riddle of "bi-location"—scientific impossibility which nevertheless seems to happen from time to time.